SOUND
MIXING
TIPS AND TRICKS

Eddie Bazil

PC Publishing

PC Publishing
Keeper's House
Merton
Thetford
Norfolk IP25 6QH
UK

Tel +44 (0)1953 889900
email info@pc-publishing.com
website http://www.pc-publishing.com

First published 2008

ISBN 13: 978 1906005 047

British Library Cataloguing in Publication Data
A catalogue record for this book is available from the British Library

Printed and bound in Great Britain by Cromwell Press Group, Trowbridge, Wilts

Contents

What is a 'good' mix?

I don't think there is a single forum that I visit, that does not have at least one thread a day devoted to the subject of mixing.

The most common questions pertain to how to obtain a good mix, what are the best tools to use, why a mix sounds one way in the studio and another way in the car or at home, what makes a good mix, where does one start, how does one mix, whether there are any good tips or guides on mixing drums or vocals etc.?

I could go on but, suffice to say, mixing is possibly one of the most important subjects in the audio recording industry, and a subject that is rarely explained in laymen's terms.

What is usually offered in terms of tutorials are ridiculous 'frequency' charts, that help no one and are so general that anyone could invent a chart in the ball park frequency range of any given instrument, and still be relatively accurate. Or super-technical script on what a particular piece of equipment offers in terms of features, but no actual hands-on experience of the use of the equipment in a studio scenario. Or, even more distressing, a huge list of expensive esoteric equipment that very few modest producers can afford. Also, in the useless advice section, goes the famous 'Apply these following settings to your bass track and it will sound meaty and great and be perfect in the mix'. What utter rubbish!

- These are all subjective, and often not very helpful.
- Every situation is unique and warrants its own solutions.

What I try to achieve in my tutorials is a hands-on approach with emphasis on visual and audio representation of the tutorial's content.

I then marry this experience with examples of how NOT to do something and what to expect if another route is chosen, basically, advice that you can hear and see, and advice that you can apply to your OWN situation.

All figures and diagrams are estimates and unique to my own situation and setup. I can only recommend techniques and data that I feel have a more universal reference, so that you too can enjoy the benefits of what I know.

Another area that seems to be debated regularly is that of 'talent' or 'having an ear'. Of course, as with any talent, it helps if you have an ear for sound, but it is not a 'must have' requirement. You can train yourself to listen better and more accurately, but more importantly, if you understand the techniques and tools required in creating a good mix, then that will suffice. Never feel as if it is not worth the hassle to learn how to mix.

The process of learning how to mix will aid you in other areas of music technology. This can only be a good thing.

I know lots of producers that do not have an ear for music but are excellent at what they do. They have trained their ears to recognize what can be deemed as a good mix. The same analogy can be made for car drivers. There are drivers that have a talent for driving and pick it up quickly, and there are drivers that have no talent but once they learn how to drive, they are then able to drive.

But before we can even contemplate on the mixing process, we need to understand what constitutes a 'good' mix. This is not a grey area and not in the least bit confusing, or up for debate. A good mix is actually quite easy to define. Obtaining a good mix is another story entirely.

What elements qualify a mix as 'good'?

1 Cleanliness
2 Clarity
3 Separation
4 Level
5 Balance (both frequency content and stereo field)
6 Genre test
7 Environment test

It's that simple. The above is a simple list of criteria that must be fulfilled before a mix can be labeled as 'good'. But, hang on, is that all there is to it? In terms of defining the attributes of a good mix, yes it is. In terms of defining a good mix for the genre it is aimed at, it still is, but with additional factors to consider and implement. We will cover this particular area later in this book.

So, let's cover the above in a little more detail.

Cleanliness

All tracks in the mix must be clean, with no noise or any anomalous artifacts. No hiss, no noise, no clicks, no pops etc, basically nothing else that does not constitute as part of the recorded audio on any given track.

The final mix must be devoid of the above.

Clarity

The audio must be clear to hear. No mushiness (or wooly effect) in the recorded audio, no particular bias to any form of EQ, nothing that can hinder you in the event that you need to dynamically treat the audio.

The final mix must be clear and not display any of the above. A mushy mix is as bad as a mix that is too rich in high frequencies. All instruments/voices must be clear to hear.

Separation

Each and every track must clearly display separation. No bleeding (audio spillage from one channel to another) must exist. No mess of shared frequencies and no clashes of frequencies must exist. Each channel must sound distinct and separate from the next/all track/s. The final mix must display good separation in the sound components used.

Level

No track must exhibit too much quietness or too much loudness, as this will be difficult to dynamically treat. All tracks must be set to nominal values and with a good S/N (signal to noise) ratio.

The final mix must display a good level that does not tire the listener. Any boosts in certain frequency ranges will tire the listener, and prove problematic on certain playing mediums.

Balance

There should be a good balance of frequency content in the mix so as not to tire the listener or to cause problems when playing the mix through other mediums (club monitors, car hi-fi etc.).

The final mix must not have any bias towards either side of the stereo field and must be sensibly spread with attention to frequency management.

Genre test

The mix should be mixed with the genre in mind. This is absolutely crucial if the mix is to be successful in it's marketplace. The final mix should appeal to the genre it is aimed at.

Environment test

The mix must sound acceptable in all environments, primarily, car hi-fi systems, home systems, studio and club systems. Whereas mastering will cover these areas in terms of presentation and the final product, it is essential that the mix fulfill the criteria listed above, so that anyone who needs to listen to the mix can do so in any environment.

The final mix should not be bias in any particular frequency range so as not to restrict the listener to a given environment.

The above are the basic criteria for a good mix, but within those criteria exist all the other important factors that are needed to be fulfilled for the mix to be deemed as 'good'.

Equally important, and one that many overlook, is the area of recording. If your source material is good to start with, then your job of mixing is made much simpler, more accurate and more enjoyable. The above list goes a long way in incorporating this thinking.

The subject of recording is a huge exercise in itself, and best left for another time. What I am trying to achieve in this particular book is to show you that you can become fluent in the techniques of mixing. Note I use the word mixing and not producing. I feel the role of the producer has been completely misunderstood in today's age and that more and more people are using this title as if it were a prerequisite to understanding how to mix, and nothing more.

We have quite clearly defined roles in this industry and the role of the engineer and producer has now been blurred into the all encompassing 'producer'. I often see youngsters, and even well known artistes, using the term 'beat producer' as the equivalent of someone who produces a track or album, or even vice versa, a beat programmer being labeled as a 'producer'. This I find belittles the roles of the engineer and producer.

If accuracy is what you are after, then you need to be very clear about the roles and qualifications of the people involved in this industry. By qualifications I do not mean college degrees etc, but someone who is qualified to perform a certain task that they are trained to perform, and in which they are experienced.

We have PA engineers, studio engineers and multimedia engineers, post production engineers, mix engineers...zzzzzzzzzzz.

The same list can be applied for producers. My job here is not to define these roles but to afford the reader the knowledge and experience required to mix a track successfully and truthfully.

So, we now have an idea as to what constitutes a good mix.

We can proceed by tackling the categories in the list and hope that that will be sufficient. It won't be.

For you to understand how to mix and actually perform the task and hear the result as you hoped, you will need to calibrate your setup and prepare the listening environment, so that what you hear is exactly what is being treated, and the final result should not be a surprise but exactly what you expected it to be.

I cannot stress how important this is. It is actually more important than any knowledge you can gain in terms of using the tools for mixing. It is the one most important factor that governs all areas of our industry. Without a 'correct' listening environment, no task can be truthfully processed. So, we now have a framework to get us started.

The first, and most important chapter, is going to kick off with preparing the listening environment.

Tip

Mastering engineers will spend more time and money in preparing and constructing their listening environment, than they will spend on any tool that they will ever need. Take this as Bible.

Tip

If you have any difficulty in understanding some of the terminology or content within this book, then please read my free online tutorials on sound, or any relevant subject matter that you may find confusing (at www.samplecraze.com).

Info

All audio examples contained within this book are available for download at the following url:

http://www.samplecraze.com/sound-mixing/

It is important to download and audition these audio files in the order that they appear in within this book.

Preparing the listening environment

I do not want to get into serious sound reinforcement or acoustic treatment here, for the very simple reason that it is a vast subject and one that is so subjective, that even pros debate it all day, with differing views.

I also believe that every room has it's own unique problems and must be treated as such, instead of offering a carte blanche solution that would probably make things worse.

However, to fully understand what needs to be done to a room to make it more accurate for listening purposes, requires that we understand how sound works in a given space, and how we perceive it within that space.

I think a good place to start, without getting technical, is to think of a room that is completely flat in terms of a flat amplitude response.

This would mean the room has almost no reflective qualities and would invariably be too dead for our purposes. The other side of the coin is a room that is too reflective, and that would be worse than a completely dead room.

We need to concentrate on a happy compromise and a realistic scenario.

Tip

What we are trying to achieve is to utilize the room's natural reflective qualities, and find ways to best expose audio, whilst beating the reflective battle. Whoa, deep statement…

To put it more simply: we are trying to limit the interference of the room with speaker placement and listening position.

The way we determine the location of sound in a given space is by measuring, with our brains, the delay of the sound between our ears. If the sound reaches the left ear first, then our brain determines that the sound is coming from the left. If there is no delay and the sound arrives at both ears at the same time, then we know that the sound is directly in front of us.

This piece of information is crucial in locating sounds and understanding the space they occupy.

Now, imagine a room that has loads of reflections and reflections that come from different angles, and at different time intervals. You can see why this would provide both confusing and inaccurate data for our brains to analyze.

Sound waves

Let us have a very brief look at how sound travels, and how we measure its effectiveness. Take a frequency travel scenario and try to explain its movement in a room. For arguments sake, let's look at a bass frequency of 60 Hz. When emitting sound, the speakers will vibrate at a rate of 60 times per second. In each cycle the speaker cones will extend forward when transmitting the sound, and retract back (rarefaction) when recoiling for the next cycle.

These vibrations create peaks on the forward drive and troughs on the refraction. Each peak and trough equates to one cycle. Imagine 60 of these every second. We can now calculate the wave cycles of this 60 Hz wave.

Sound travels at approximately 1130 feet per second, so we can calculate how many wave cycles that is for the 60 Hz wave. We divide 1130 by 60, and the result is around 19 feet (18.83 if you want to be anal about it).

We can now deduce that each wave cycle is 19 feet apart. To calculate each half cycle, i.e. the distance between the peak and trough, drive and rarefaction, we simply divide by two.

We now have a figure of 9.5 feet. What that tells us is that if you sat anywhere up to 9.5 feet from your speakers, the sound would fly past you completely flat. However, this is assuming you have no boundaries of any sort in the room, i.e. no walls or ceiling.

We know that to be impossible, so we then need to factor in the boundaries. Are you still with me here? These boundaries will reflect back the sound from the speakers and get mixed with the original source sound.

Reflected sounds

This is not all that happens. The reflected sounds can come from different angles and because of their 'bouncing' nature; they could come at a different time to other waves. And because the reflected sound gets mixed with the source sound, the actual volume of the mixed wave is louder.

In certain parts of the room, the reflected sound will amplify because a peak might meet another peak (constructive interference), and in other parts of the room where a peak meets a trough (rarefaction), frequencies are cancelled out (destructive interference).

Calculating what happens where is a nightmare. This is why your mix will sound poor.

It is crucial for our ears to hear the sound from the speakers before they hear the reflected sounds. For argument's sake, I will call this sound 'primary' or 'leading', and the reflective sound 'secondary' or 'following'.

So, by eliminating as many of the secondary (reflective) sounds as possible, we leave the brain with the primary sound to deal with. This will allow for a more accurate location of the sound, and a better representation of the frequency content.

But is this what we really want? I ask this, because the secondary sound is also important in a 'real' space and goes to form the tonality of the sound being heard. Words like rich, tight, full etc. all come from secondary sounds (reflected).

So, we don't want to completely remove them as this would then give us a clinically dead space. We want to keep certain secondary sounds and only diminish the ones that really interfere with the sound.

Our brains also have the ability to filter or ignore unwanted frequencies. In the event that the brain is bombarded with too many reflections, it will have a problem localizing the sounds, so it decides to ignore, or suppress, them. The best example of this is when there is a lot of noise about you, like in a room or a bar, and you are trying to have a conversation with someone. The brain can ignore the rest of the noise and focus on 'hearing' the conversation you are trying to have. I am sure you have experienced this in public places, parties, clubs, football matches etc.

Reflective surfaces

To carry that over to our real world situation of a home studio, we need to understand that reflective surfaces will create major problems, and the most common of these reflective culprits are walls.

However, there is a way of overcoming this, assuming the room is not excessively reflective, and is the standard bedroom/living room type of space with carpet and curtains.

We overcome this with clever speaker placement and listening position, and before you go thinking that this is just an idea and not based on any scientific foundation, think again. *The idea is to have the primary sound arrive at our ears before the secondary sound.*

Walls are the worst culprits, but because we know that sound travels at a given speed, we can make sure that the primary sound will reach our ears before the secondary sound does. By doing this, and with the Haas effect, our brains will prioritize the primary sound and suppress (if at low amplitude) the secondary sound, which will have the desired result, albeit not perfectly.

Some frequencies will be reinforced, others suppressed, thus altering the character of the sound. Curtains and carpets will absorb certain frequencies, but not all, so it can sometimes be more damaging than productive. For this, we need to understand the surfaces that exist in the room.

In our home studio scenario, we are assuming that a carpet and curtains, plus the odd sofa etc, are all that are in the room. We are not dealing with a steel factory floor studio.

In any listening environment, what we hear is a result of a mixture of both the primary and secondary (reflected) sounds. We know this to be true and our sound field will be a combination of both.

The trick is to place the speaker in a location that will take of advantage of the desirable reflections, while diminishing the unwanted reflections.

Speaker positioning

Distance to side wall and back wall

Most speakers need to be a minimum of a foot or two away from the side and back walls to reduce early reflections. Differences among speakers can also influence positioning, so you must always read the manufacturer's specification before starting to position the speakers. A figure-of-eight pattern may be less critical of a nearby side wall, but very critical of the distance to the back wall.

The reverse is true for dynamic speakers that exhibit cardioid patterns. In

> **Tip**
>
> A room affects the sound of a speaker by the reflections it causes.

> **Tip**
>
> Solid surfaces will reflect and porous surfaces will absorb, but this is all highly reliant on the materials being used.

> **Tip**
>
> In general, the primary sound, from the speakers, is responsible for the image, while the secondary sounds contribute to the tonality of the received sound.

general, the further away from reflective surfaces, the better.

It is also crucial to keep the distances from the back wall and side walls mismatched. If your speakers are set 3 feet from the back wall, do NOT place them 3 feet from the side walls, place them at a different distance.

Another crucial aspect of the listening position and speaker placement is that the distance from your listening position to each speaker be absolutely identical. It has been calculated that an error of less than half an inch can affect the speaker sound imaging, so get this absolutely correct.

Distance to speakers from listening position

Once you have established the above, you now need to sort out the distance from the listener to the speakers. I work off an equilateral triangle with the seating position being at the apex of this triangle. The distances must all be equal.

The other factor to consider is the distance between the speakers. Too close and you will get a narrow soundstage with the focus being very central. Widening the distance between the speakers will afford you a wider stereo width, but too far and you will lose the integrity of the soundstage.

Toe-in

This is the angle of the speakers facing the listener. There are a number of factors that influence the angle of the speakers. The room, the speakers themselves, and your preferred listening angle. I always start at an excessive toe-in and work outwards until I can hear the soundstage perfectly.

Tilt

Tilt is also crucial. Depending on the make of the speakers, most speakers are meant to be level set, but some might require tilting and in most cases, the tilt is rear high. If you have to have the speakers tilted then start off level and work from there. Personally I prefer a level speaker setup.

Listening height

The optimum listening height is that when the speaker's centre is at exactly ear height. However, certain speakers have their own specific height recommendations. You will find that with 3-way systems that incorporate top, mid and sub woofers, the listening height is more customized to account for the woofer placements in the speaker cabin or housing.

Seating location

I find that keeping the seating position 1-3 feet from the boundary wall gives me the best bass response, and because the distance is too short for the brain to measure the time delay and thus locate the source of the reflection (Figure 2.1).

The listening position is at the rear of the room with the speakers facing and forming the equilateral triangle setup, and the listening position forming the apex of the triangle. The elliptical shape denotes the soundstage and as you can plainly see, the side and rear walls do not interfere with the soundstage.

As you can see, I have created this soundstage using the longer walls as

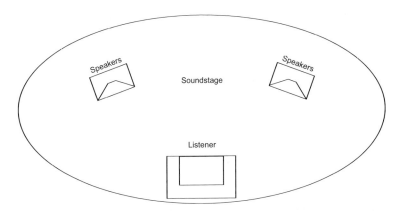

Figure 2.1
The listening position is at the rear of the room with the speakers facing and forming the equilateral triangle setup, and the listening position forming the apex of the triangle.

Tip

Please make sure to take care in optimizing your listening environment. Once this has been achieved, you can mix far more accurately and truthfully.

the back and front walls, instead of creating the soundstage with the listening position on the shorter walls. This allows me to position the speakers as wide as is sonically possible and thus affording me a wider stereo field.

Place the listening chair near the rear wall, because the distance (1 to 3 feet) is too short for the brain to measure the time delay and locate the source of the reflection. Also, it places you at the room boundary where the perception of bass is greatest.

We can now move onto the subject of calibration.

Calibrating the signal path

For you to achieve an accurate mix, you need to calibrate your signal path to show a consistent value throughout the signal path.

The signal strength at the input stage should match, exactly, the signal strength at the output stage. This is called Unity Gain. What this basically means is that if you input a value of, say, 3dB, then you should see and hear that same value right through your signal path to the output: 3dB in, 3dB out.

Double standards

If you input that 3dB value as a synthesizer gain (synthesizer's output level) through your mixer's input/s, then through the master stereo outs (or sub groups) of the mixer, into the sound card, and finally through the master outs in your sequencing software, then you should see and hear the same value of 3dB. This is what you would think, right?

It isn't that simple I'm afraid, and the reason being is that we have different standards in the audio industry. As far as analogue signal levels are concerned, though, there are only two to worry about: +4dBu and -10dBV, respectively the professional and semi-professional standards. But what do these levels actually represent?

The reference point in any decibel scale is always 0dB and a suffix letter is used to denote the chosen standard.

In an analogue mixer, a test level signal of 0VU on the output meters means that the main outputs should measure +4dBu. That is the pro level standard, which means we can align input and output levels to exhibit unity gain throughout a signal chain. In other words, you can pass signals between equipment and know that you won't overload anything or disappear into the noise floor.

Tip

As far as analogue signal levels are concerned, though, there are only two standards to worry about: +4dBu and -10dBV, respectively the professional and semi-professional standards

Info

Notice that I am avoiding using any maths or physics to explain these measurements and standards. This book has been written with the layman in mind, not the technician. If you want to mesmerize yourself and read the technical specifications and the maths, then there are some excellent articles on this subject. For the sake of our calibration chapter, I am only interested in supplying you with working figures.

Info

Digital systems cannot record audio of greater amplitude than the maximum quantising level.

Tip

Bearing in mind that the industry standard for 'Red Book' specification for audio CDs insists that material should peak above -4dBFS, then you can see why 0dBFS peaking is crucial.

Tip

In the digital domain, you can kiss gain pushing goodbye. 0 is max, that is Gospel.

The semi-pro level standard of -10dBV was adopted for unbalanced signal interfaces using much simpler (or cheaper) circuitry. The standard -10dBV level equates to about a quarter of the voltage of the professional +4dBu reference level, or almost 12dB lower.

Most professional systems are designed to handle peak levels in the region of +22dBu. +28dBu is very good, while +18dB is pretty standard on budget equipment; therefore, working off the pro nominal signal value of +4dBu, with the maximum peak level being +22dBu, we have 18dB of headroom in the system.

This is simple to calculate, and always keep that simple calculation in mind when you buy a piece of gear, and the manufacturer boasts its spec claims. You now know how to calculate the headroom required on any system.

How does that equate to the reading on the mixer? Well, you have to be aware that almost all analogue mixers, that follow a VU metering system, never show the 'true' scale peak value, but the average.

What this means in the real world, is that although the VU meters will show, say 6 dB above 0, the actual figure is well above that, usually by as much as 6 dB. This is because VU meters are not instant metering tools, and react to average values.

For music hitting the +10 LED on peak-reading meters, the true signal peaks will be reaching the +20dBu mark (+14dBu plus 6dB overshoot), which is only 2dB below clipping in a typical system.

A mixer will often have enough headroom, and usually around the 10 dB mark, for the user to be able to 'drive' the signal past 0 dB and still have no distortion. Of course, gain pushing on analogue mixers is a technique used for getting more 'warmth' out of a mix; by driving past 0 dB. Another funky tip, but alas, shows how old school I am.

Now let's look at the digital side of this. Digital systems cannot record audio of greater amplitude than the maximum quantising . The digital signal reference point as at the top of the digital meter scale is 0dBFS, FS standing for 'full scale'.

Since analogue equipment provides around 18dB or more of headroom, it seems sensible to configure digital systems in the same way. In the US, the adopted standard of setting the nominal analogue level is: 0dBu equals -20dBFS, thereby tolerating peaks of up to 20 dBu. In Europe, 0dBu equals to -18dBFS, thereby tolerating peaks of up to +18dBu.

This all sounds complicated but all you really need to be concerned with, as far as the digital world is concerned, is that we have a peak meter scale of 0 dBFS. Beyond this you have clipping and distortion.

Bearing in mind that the industry standard for 'Red Book' specification for audio CDs insists that material should peak above -4dBFS, then you can see why 0dBFS peaking is crucial.

The problem for most semi pro and project studios is that the vast majority of A/D converters are already adjusted to accommodate the headroom, as discussed earlier, according to the international standards.

Using +4dBu as the standard, this will produce a -16dBFS digital signal. So, the analogue mixer's peak levels will register +12dBu (+8VU), but will only achieve peak digital levels of about -8dBFS. Without any form of dynamic gain boost, this level will sound too quiet.

This is where calibration comes into the equation. I can honestly say that out of every 10 studios I visit, home or semi-pro, 8 are not calibrated.

How often have you created a mix, then played it in your car/home hi-fi system, only to find it is either too quiet or so loud that it distorts?

Another advantage of signal path calibration is that of 'balance'. By going through the calibration process, you will invariably sort out any bias problems that you may be experiencing with the stereo imaging. Bias of either side of the stereo field is as damaging as an inaccurate signal path value.

What we are trying to achieve is a clean and strong audio signal, equal in value right throughout the signal path, and showing no bias to either side of the stereo field.

This may sound complicated but in practice it is actually quite simple.

The procedure

If you have a mixer's outputs connected directly to your sound card's inputs, then you need to start right at the input stage of the mixer.

If you do not have a mixer and are going directly into the sound card's inputs, then follow this procedure as well, but substituting the sound card's inputs as the direct input stage.

You need to input a line level signal into one of the input channels on the mixer. I always recommend a constant, non fluctuating signal, like a sine test tone at 1 kHz, or any sound that is constant, sustaining and not dynamically fluctuating. Avoid sounds that have variety in their waveforms, like drum loops or evolving pad sounds etc.

We need a constant single level input signal, like a sustaining sine bass sound, or a constant raw waveform, but not noise.

Flatten the mixer

But first, you need to 'flatten' (flatline) the mixer. This basically means that you turn all faders down, all pan pots to centre, all auxiliaries and inserts to off/zero, remove all EQs by depressing them or turning them down to centre where there is no cut or boost, depress phantom power, and finally, turn the input gain knob on the mixer's channel, that you are inputting the tone through, to zero. We now have a flatlined mixer.

Most mixer faders start at 0 for Unity, and can be moved down or up. We need to put the channel's fader at 0 and the mixer's main stereo outs faders to 0. We are trying to achieve a signal value of 0dB, because we know that equates to +4 dBu (pro standard).

Make sure your monitors (speakers) are connected to the mixer and on, and that your mixer's monitor outs (control room or main mix or master outs etc.) are on and at a level that you can hear the monitors.

Now start to raise the input knob (trim) on the input channel until you have a level showing on the meter or LED. Your input signal should be bang on at 0, and the master outs metering should be bang on 0VU. Do not adjust the faders for the input channel and master outs. You need to set your input level using the input channel's gain/trim knob. This is called Unity Gain.

Calibrate the sound card

We now need to calibrate the sound card. Check the control panel of the software that came with the sound card and check to see what the level is going into the computer. The control panel will probably have faders for controlling levels going into and out of the sound card. Select the 'audio in' fader and set this to 0, as you did with the mixer.

We know that in the digital domain the input level should be -16 dBFS, as discussed earlier. You need to decide what level of adjustment you need to make. I prefer to use a value close to commercial CD standard, of about -2 dB.

For me; I adjust the input level to around -14 dBFS, which allows me the headroom to peak at -2 dBFS. I do this because I know I can push the mixer to + 10 dB before I experience any distortion, and in the digital domain that would be my peak value of -2 dBFS. In other words, I am accommodating the headroom with a setting of -14 dBFS.

If you wanted bang on 0 dB, then you can adjust the input on the A/D (soundcard) to be exactly that, but you run the risk of clipping beyond 0 dBFS in the event that the material being input peaks beyond 0.

You need to calibrate your system based on what your A/D is doing in the digital domain. It's always good practice to record and test a signal after you have completed the calibration. If you find that your recording is too loud or too quiet, then you need to adjust the input level accordingly.

The D/A setting

Now we need to sort out the replay end of things. This is the D/A setting. We know that 0 dBFS in the digital domain equates to +20 dBu on the analogue mixer (using pro standard of +4 dBu). That is way too loud and will distort the signal.

If you have control over the D/A output, then setting this to 0VU on the analogue mixer is important for proper calibration. Commercially recorded music needs to be aligned by using the following signal: -8dBFS to align with +4dBu or 0VU.

Personally, I prefer to have the same input and output values right through the A/D D/A, so that unity is shown both at input and output.

If there is a discrepancy at the input or output stage, then adjust the sound card's respective gain knobs, but checking with the control panel to make sure there is no clipping etc.

Once you have set up the right listening environment and calibrated your signal path, then you are in a position of strength. Hearing exactly what is being mixed, right from input to final output, in a room with no bias towards certain frequencies, will allow for a much more accurate and precise mix. It will also make the whole mixing experience much more enjoyable.

I often find that mixing in the right environment, and with a calibrated signal path, affords me more creative ideas as I know I am mixing from a position of strength, and do not need to worry about the mix sounding one way in the room and another way on a hi-fi system, or in my car.

This confidence makes me more assertive in trying different things out. It also saves me so much time in having to correct bad sound representations

---

Tip

You need to calibrate your system based on what your A/D is doing in the digital domain. It's always good practice to record and test a signal after you have completed the calibration. If you find that your recording is too loud or too quiet, then you need to adjust the input level accordingly.

Info

Commercially recorded music needs to be aligned by using the following signal: -8dBFS to align with +4dBu or 0VU.

that I allocate the time saved to trying out different versions of the same mix.

Chapters 1 and 2 are probably the most important factors in attaining a good mix. It does not matter how much knowledge or talent you possess. If the room isn't right, the sound isn't right.

Now let us move on to the next stage of this book: Personal preparation.

Tip

It does not matter how much knowledge or talent you possess. If the room isn't right, the sound isn't right.

Personal preparation

This probably sounds like a hygiene course, but it's not. This is about all the other little things you can do to give you the best possible chance of performing a good mix. You would be surprised at how little things can affect a good mix.

Let's kick off with the most important.

Ears

Your ears are quite amazing. They are, without a doubt, the most important tools you have at your disposal when it comes to ANY audio work.

However, you need to attune your ears, and brain, to corrective listening, so as to attain the best possible mix. The brain has an uncanny ability to store information and use that information for referencing. In this instance, you need to listen to a well produced piece of audio, so that your ears and brain can attune themselves to the dynamic qualities of the well produced piece of audio. By doing this, your brain registers these qualities and uses it as a reference guide.

I always recommend to my students that they listen to well produced audio for about 15-20 minutes, prior to starting the mix process. This allows the brain to register the dynamic qualities of the well produced audio, and then to compare the mix qualities with this. I also advise that the music chosen for this be music that is similar in genre. So, if you are mixing a classical track, it makes sense to listen to a classical piece and listen out for the way it is presented etc. It does not make sense to listen to a thrash metal track. The same is true for any genre.

Even after many years, I still go through this procedure. You cannot believe how much it will aid you in your mix. Try it!

Lighting

Make sure the lighting in the studio is conducive to the mix process. But also make sure that you have enough light to see detail in editing etc.

I like to use soft and dimmed lighting if I am mixing a ballad and stronger, brighter lighting if I am mixing a club track. This sets the mood for me.

I have always believed that if you try to mimic the environment that the final mix will be listened in, then you have the mindset to perform a better mix as you will 'feel' as if you are in the final listening environment. Of course, this is highly subjective and down to the individual's personal preference. I can only speak for myself.

Well ventilated room

This is very important as the more CO_2 you breathe in, the more lethargic and sleepy you will feel. This will have an adverse effect on the mixing process. Fresh air will keep you alert and feeling energetic. It will also help in keeping the equipment cool, or rather, cooler.

Hardware studio equipment that involves amps and transformers generates a lot of heat. Warm rooms tend to make me sleepy, so I always try to keep my studio a little cooler than normal.

Making sure there is a good airflow in the studio is important in keeping temperatures down to tolerable levels, and in keeping you alert and fresh.

Cleanliness

As with all things that are mindset dependent, keeping the studio clean and organized will have a positive effect on the mind and thus the mix. Clean surfaces, sensible cabling and an organized room, not only help you in the actual physical process of working, but also help the mind in thinking clearly and unconfused.

Tip

No drugs, no alcohol, is a given. Keep it clean, keep it clear.

No drugs or alcohol

There is no better way to guarantee a bad mix. I don't need to go into deep explanations about perception, hearing, vision, emotion etc. However, make sure you have plenty of water or juice handy. As with fresh air, liquids are also important in maintaining a healthy and fresh mindset.

The task at hand

Make sure to prepare the studio for the mix. Have all your hardware dynamics and effects patched in, ready for the mix. The same is true for software.

Prepare everything for the mix prior to the mix process itself, as having to get up and patch in a dynamic during the mixing process will interfere with the train of thought and 'feel'.

Tip

Make notes about the tools and settings used.

It is also helpful to make notes about the tools and settings used. In the event that you need to postpone the mix for another time, you can easily recall the tools used and their settings.

The more you prepare, the easier the mixing process.

Don't mix in one sitting

Try to complete the mix over a few days, or to take long breaks during the mixing. This will neutralize the ears, and mind, and you will listen with fresh ears and thus perform a better and more accurate mix.

I find that getting away from the mix and coming back to it on another day gives me the advantage of starting again with a new perspective and with fresh ears. I am not suggesting redoing the whole mix, but to listen to it again and fine tune it. I often find that this is one of the most important influences in performing a good mix.

Comfort

If you can, wear comfortable clothes, and sit in a well padded and comfortable chair with good back support. This will help you greatly on long sessions and the more comfortable you are the less you worry about having to get up and stretch your limbs, or to remove certain bits of clothing as they have become constricting.

Allocate time and no distractions

I like to allocate a certain amount of time to a mix and then move onto something else. This gives me time to rest my senses and to get away from the monotony of the same track.

Have you noticed that the longer you spend on the same track, the worse or confusing it starts to sound? This is because your ears and brain get used to certain frequencies and thus start to ignore them, and that they get irritated by other frequencies and try to filter them. So, you try to boost the signals your ears have come to abate, and diminish the frequencies that have started to hurt your ears.

Distractions do not help the mix process either. Telephones are the most common culprits, be it mobile or land line. Distractions interfere with the thought process and affect the mix.

Of course there are distractions that cannot be helped. Food and toilet spring to mind.

Tip

Have you noticed that the longer you spend on the same track, the worse or confusing it starts to sound? This is because your ears and brain get used to certain frequencies and thus start to ignore them, and that they get irritated by other frequencies and try to filter them.

Tip

Take a break.

The tools

Your listening environment is now ready. Your signal path is now calibrated. You are mentally and physically ready to mix.

So, what is left? The tools of course: knowing what to use and when to use them. These tools are also known as 'Signal Processors', because ... they process the audio signal ... sigh.

But before we jump in at the deep end, let us first, briefly examine what these tools are.

Almost all the tools you will use in mixing are categorized into the following two categories:

1 Effects
2 Dynamics

There are, of course, other tools such as dithering plug-ins, sample rate converters etc., but these are tools for audio management and reformats, and fall under mastering or 'project requirements'. What we are concerned with are the actual tools used in the mix process, and not after.

Effects

Effects are excellent sculpting tools and a number of genres today have made their mark because of the types of effects used within the genre.

* Trance would be a good example of the use of delays and reverbs.
* Distortion is prevalent in the Rock genres etc.

Effects can be used globally on the whole mix, or individually on single tracks or events, or in a combination of both (reverbs for example).

Effects can be used creatively to evoke an emotion, or, for example, correctively to encompass space where space is lacking. In the former, a big reverb on strings can result in the strings sounding huge and warm, or bright and exploding. In the latter, sensible use of reverb can add space to a certain sound in a mix that sounds too dry compared to the surrounding instruments that may have been recorded with space.

It is limitless what can be achieved with effects. You are limited only by your imagination, and of course, which tools you own.

Chaining effects can lead to dramatic results. However, soft and subtle use of effects can result in track strengthening qualities. Using a chorus on a bass sound can thicken the bass. Adding a slight amount of delay to vocals can make the vocals sound fuller and deeper.

Understanding how best to utilize an effect is reliant on understanding the mechanics of the effect, what it does and how it works, and in what quantities to use it for optimum results.

Let us now take a brief look at the most common effects and how they work.

Reverb

This is the biggie and the most common effect used in music. We have been listening to music acoustically, for thousands of years. Space has been determined by the environment.

The listener hears the original sound, plus all the reflected sounds that come from the original sound reflecting, and re-reflecting, off the environment's surfaces. As a result, the listener hears a composite of the original audio signal, the first reflections, and the delayed reflections. These 'signals' will eventually lose their energy and dissipate.

The environment itself, as we have seen earlier, has a dramatic effect on the signal's characteristics. High frequencies are more prone to absorption and rooms with absorbing materials (curtains, carpets etc.) will sound more muffled. Rooms with hard reflective surfaces will sound brighter and more brittle. Today, we emulate the space of the environment and use this in our music.

Our effects units can not only emulate real room spaces but also create spaces that do not exist naturally in nature, like gated reverbs or reverse reverbs.

Figure 4.1 displays what happens to the signal being treated. There is a pre delay just before the signal reflects. (The time taken for the signal to reach and reflect from the first surface is known as pre delay.) In other words, the pre delay controls the amount of time before the reverb sound begins. By adjusting this parameter you can impress a change in distance.

Think about it. The longer it takes for a sound to reach a reflecting surface, the further that reflective surface is away from the sound source. This is then followed by the early reflections. The decay time denotes how long it takes for the reverb sound to dissipate, or die.

In most reverb units you will have a high frequency roll-off, sometimes referred to as HF damp. In natural spaces high frequencies dissipate quicker than low frequencies. By controlling this roll-off we can simulate the frequency dissipation.

As Figure 4.1 clearly shows, there are a number of early reflections spaced out between each other. This is where diffusion comes into the equation. Diffusion parameters control the spacing in between the early reflections. The tighter they are packed together, the thicker the sound, and vice versa. By applying more diffusion, you tighten the gaps and the reflections pack together tighter and thus the thickened sound.

If you apply less diffusion, the opposite happens; you space out the reflections further apart and make for a thinner reverb sound.

I bet no one has ever bothered to explain that to you in such a simple way? Pah, humbug I say … humbug!

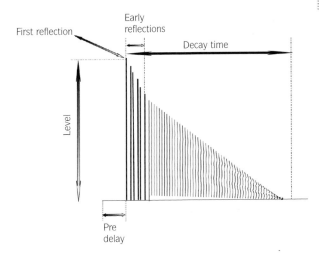

First reflection

Early reflections

Decay time

Level

Pre delay

Figure 4.1
The various parameters of reverb.

Mix, or wet/dry, denotes mixing the dry signal with the treated wet signal (the reverb signal). This is self explanatory. The more 'mix' you apply the wetter the signal becomes. In other words the more 'mix' you apply, the more reverb you apply to the dry signal.

Today's software reverbs carry even more editing options and these are often reflected (no pun) by the different parameters they offer. However, I would rather touch on the subject of convolution reverbs.

Convolution reverb

Basically, a specially recorded sample (containing the impulse response) of a real acoustic reverberation pattern is imposed on ('convolved with') another audio signal. The result is a reverberant signal with many of the sonic characteristics of the original acoustic space.

This technology is now leaping in bounds, ahead of most software based reverb plugins. The fact that you can sample the presets off a Lexicon 480, or an Eventide H3000, and use it in your software convolution plug-in, is astounding and highly desirable.

However, the very nature of the process means that your CPU is munching away hungrily. This process is very CPU intensive and so limits the use of the plug-in to either a global stereo effect or small instances on very few tracks. I am sure in the future this will become a mere memory, as computer technology and power advances.

Delay

A delay unit takes an input signal, holds it then plays it back after a specified time. Delay is the time interval between the input signal and its repetition at the output of the delay device. Depending on the time intervals and nature of the delay, many varying effects can be created.

In addition to this, you can have a number of parameters that perform different functions. There will be a facility to mix the delayed (wet) signal with the dry signal, and usually the option to 'feed' the delayed signal back into the input stage. This is called feedback.

Tip

Delay is the time interval between the input signal and its repetition at the output of the delay device.

Modulation, a varying of the delay time over a particular range is another key parameter of time based delays. By assigning minimum and maximum values, the delay time will sweep between the two and create a 'moving' delay as the times vary over the set range. You can also 'tap' a delay time into some of the more modern delay units. This can create some unique time delays and allows the user more control over the time.

Different amounts of time delays give different effects.

0-15 ms (milliseconds)

Mixing a delay of this time creates an effect called flanging. This effect imparts a phasing type of effect, much akin to a jet plane going by. Great for guitars and drums.

10-25 ms

This accounts for a chorus effect. This effect sounds like two identical instruments playing together, full bodied and moving. Great for adding depth and width to a bass sound.

25-50 ms

This is the stage when the delay enters the land of echo, whereby you hear the sound being repeated. Between 30-80 ms, the echo is denoted as 'slapback'. Great for basses and even vocals.

50 ms and up

This is where true echo takes place, whereby an instrument sounds doubled up. Once we go beyond the 300 ms mark, the delay starts to sound very distinct and can be manipulated to add ambiance.

Most of today's delays are BPM synced, have LFO controls, filters etc. and are very detailed and useful, and this level of control marks it as a great tool for producers and musicians alike.

Delay is one seriously great effect. You can create vibrato with it, emulate speakers, create crazy pans etc. It is versatile and powerful.

Chorus

The 'shimmering' effect. Between 15-35 ms delay times.

Sweeping the delay makes the wet signal bend up and down in pitch, or detune itself. Combining the dry and wet signal together gives you chorus.

We have touched on this but I wanted to take this a step further and mention stereo chorus. In one channel, the delayed signal is combined with the dry signal in the same polarity. In the other channel, the delayed signal is inverted in polarity then combined with the dry signal. Thus the right channel has peaks in the frequency response, whereas the left channel has dips, or vice versa. This makes for a spatial and wide chorus effect.

Flange

0-20 ms of delay time. At this time delay, you cannot resolve the dry and wet signals into separate sounds. As described earlier, you hear a single sound but with phase. The two signals combine and have phase interference, which puts a series of dips and peaks in the frequency response. This is the comb-filter type of effect and gives a sound similar to the filter equivalent.

For me, these are the primary effects I always use. Of course there are many others, and most are variations of the above. Effects like harmonizers, distortion, tube simulators etc. are all extremely useful, but for the sake of this book, I am only concerned with the above. Once you understand these basic effects, when the time comes to bring the other effects into this book, you will understand what I am talking about.

There isn't a single mix out there that does not sport some kind of effect, so take special care when using these fine tools. For vocals alone, you must understand effects, because if you don't, then the mix is sunk.

Dynamics
Possibly the most abused and misunderstood of all the tools. For the purposes of this book, I am going to concentrate only on the two main dynamics, as they are the most important of all dynamics in today's world of mixing.

I could go on about exciters, noise gates (we will touch on this later), harmonizers etc. but I think I need to be realistic and discuss the tools that will be used regularly.

In the virtual world, noise is less of an issue as far as recording goes, but is prevalent as a side effect when dynamics are used. We will tackle this when it arises.

Equalization – EQ

Types of EQ
To begin to understand the EQ, we need to first define the two categories it falls in, Passive and Active.

Passive EQs
These types of EQs have the distinction of being extremely simple in design and, more importantly, they cannot boost frequencies, only cut. The way they work is actually very much to do with perception. By cutting, for example, low frequencies (bass), they make the mid and high frequencies sound 'louder'.

Passive EQs do have their uses. Although they are inflexible, they can perform reduction tasks reasonably well. By cutting high frequencies, they are able to cut or lower hiss (high frequency noise). However, by their very nature, passive EQs, or filters, have to then have the signal boosted to compensate for the cut. This, in itself, introduces noise into the signal path. The noise coming from the amp used to boost the signal.

Active EQs
Because of the limitations of passive EQs, most EQs are built around active filter circuits which use frequency selective components, together with a low noise amplifier.

It is this type of EQ that we are now going to concentrate on.

Fixed frequency EQ

Pretty self explanatory, this EQ allows cut/boost of one or more frequencies. There are no additional controls over the usual components, like bandwidth, Q, etc.

Peaking EQ

A peaking EQ is an EQ which boosts a specific band of frequencies. Whereas a shelving filter has a shelf like curve, this filter has a bell shaped curve. The Q setting determines the width of the bell, while boost or cut determines the height or depth of the bell.

Two band or three band

These types of EQ simply have two or three separate frequency ranges. Usually denoted as low, mid and high, these bands can only be cut or boosted.

Shelving filter/EQ

We have touched on the use of tone controls that are forms of EQ. These controls control a type of filter that is called a shelving filter. In the case of the bass and treble knobs, low pass and high pass shelving filters are used respectively.

A low-pass shelving filter passes all frequencies below its cut-off frequency, but attenuates all frequencies above its cut-off frequency. Similarly, a high-pass filter passes all frequencies above its cut-off frequency, but attenuates all frequencies below its cut-off frequency.

This is the simplest type of active EQ. This EQ can shape response in a number of ways: boost/cut low frequencies, boost/cut high frequencies. This is why I have included the graph to demonstrate what happens with the filters, low and high pass, in this type of EQ.

Most mixers will allow for low and high frequency EQ, and in the case of shelving filters, their mid frequencies are usually fixed.

It is also common for the filter slope to be 6 dB per octave. This allows for a gentler effect. The shape is shelf like, so the boost or cut is progressive over a range. Filters do not have a no-effect at a frequency and then instantly jump and suddenly reappear at the next frequency. They have to get there somehow. The way, and by how much, they get there is called the gradient or slope. In the case of the shelving filter, the most common slope is 6 dB gain change per octave (doubling of the frequency). It takes time for the filter to attenuate frequencies, in proportion to the distance from the cut-off point. This is the slope.

Figures 4.2 and 4.3 illustrate what happens if you cut or boost frequencies in a low-pass and a hi-pass filter.

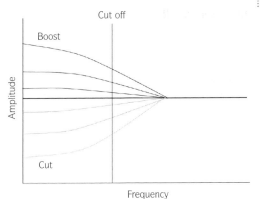

Figure 4.2
Cutting and boosting frequencies in a
low pass filter

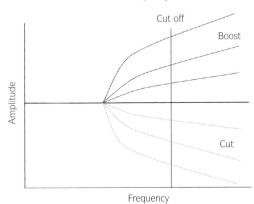

Figure 4.3
Cutting and boosting frequencies in a
high pass filter

> **Tip**
>
> A graphic equalizer is simply a set of filters, each with a fixed centre frequency that cannot be changed.

Graphic EQ

A graphic equalizer is simply a set of filters, each with a fixed centre frequency that cannot be changed. The only control you have is the amount of boost or cut in each frequency band. This boost or cut is most often controlled with sliders. The sliders are a graphic representation of the frequency response, hence the name 'graphic' equalizer. The more frequency bands you have, the more control and accuracy you have over the frequency response.

> **Tip**
>
> The more frequency bands you have, the more control and accuracy you have over the frequency response.

Mixing consoles rarely have graphic EQs, but PA mixers often have a stereo graphic EQ for EQing the final stereo output. A graphic equalizer uses a set of band-pass filters that are designed to completely isolate certain frequency bands.

Band pass filter

A filter that passes frequencies between two limits is known as a band-pass filter. This is a great filter. It attenuates frequencies below and above the cut-off and leaves the frequencies at the cut-off. It is, in effect, a low pass and a high pass together. The cool thing about this filter is that you can eliminate the lower and higher frequencies and be left with a band of frequencies that you can then use as either an effect, as in having that real mid range type of old radio sound, or use it for isolating a narrow band of frequencies in recordings that have too much low and high end.

> **Tip**
>
> Try the band pass filter on synthesizer sounds and you will come up with some wacky sounds.

Try this filter on synthesizer sounds and you will come up with some wacky sounds. It really is a useful filter and if you can run more than one at a time,

Figure 4.4
A band-pass filter attenuates frequencies below and above the cut-off and leaves the frequencies at the cut-off.

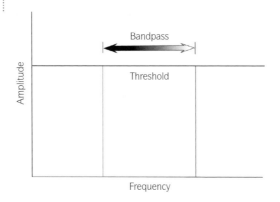

and select different cut-offs for each one, then you will get even more interesting results. Interestingly enough, band pass filtering is used on formant filters that you find on so many softsynths, plug-ins, synthesizers and samplers. Emu are known for some of their formant filters and the technology is based around band pass filters. It is also good for thinning out sounds and can be used on percussive sounds as well as creating effects types of sounds.

I often get emails from programmers wanting to know how they can get that old radio effect or telephone line chat effect or even NASA space dialogue from space to Houston. Well, this is one of the tools. Use it and experiment. You will enjoy this one.

Notch filter – also know as band reject filter

This is the exact opposite of the band pass filter. It allows frequencies below and above the cut-off and attenuates the frequencies around the cut-off point. Why is this good? Well, it eliminates a narrow band of frequencies, the frequencies around the cut-off, so, that in itself is a great tool. You can use this on all sounds and can have a distinct effect on a sound, not only in terms of eliminating the frequencies that you want eliminated, but also in terms of creating a new flavour to a sound.

But its real potency is in eliminating frequencies you don't want. Because you select the cut-off point, in essence, you are selecting the frequencies around that cut-off point and eliminating them.

An invaluable tool when you want to hone in on a band of frequencies located, for example, right in the middle of a sound or recording. I sometimes use a notch filter on drum sounds that have a muddy or heavy mid section, or on sounds that have a little noise or frequency clash in the mid section of a sound.

Parametric filter

This filter controls three parameters, frequency, bandwidth and gain. You select the range of frequencies you want to boost or cut, you select the width of that range and use the gain to boost or cut the frequencies, within the selected bandwidth, by a selected amount.

The frequencies not in the bandwidth are not altered. If you widen the bandwidth to the limit of the upper and lower frequency ranges then this is called shelving. Most parametric filters have shelving parameters.

Parametric filters are great for more complex filtering jobs and can be used to create real dynamic effects because they can attenuate or boost any range of frequencies.

Basically, the parametric EQ places several active filters across the frequency spectrum. Each filter is designated to a frequency range, low, mid, high etc. You have the usual cut/boost, resonant frequency and bandwidth. It is these qualities and the control over them that places this particular EQ in the producer's arsenal of dynamic tools, and makes it detailed and versatile. However, you need to understand what you are doing when using a parametric EQ, otherwise things can go very wrong.

Quasi-parametric EQ

This is just another form of parametric EQ but without the bandwidth control.

Sweep EQ

This is very similar to a band pass filter, but with variable centre frequency, and no control over the width of the filter response (Q).

You will find that most mixers will have band pass EQ, and some will have sweep EQ (where the centre frequency can be varied, also known as 'tuneable'), but very few, mainly digital, will have parametric EQ.

Paragraphic EQ

This is another variation on the graphic EQ. This EQ provides control over the centre frequency of each band.

Phase the bi-product

A very important aspect of EQ, in relation to affected and non-affected frequencies, is that of phase.

We know that affecting the frequencies that we have chosen for equalization also affects the phase of those selected frequencies, in relation to the unaffected frequencies. The process itself also affects the frequency response of the signal being treated. We are talking about tiny offsets here. Every time a frequency range is selected and treated, the affected frequencies will exhibit displacement, in relation to the unaffected frequencies. This offset is phase. Whereas we are not talking about big swirling phase effects, as in guitar phasing, we are, however, talking about the pure definition of phase. This is probably not something that you will hear as phase, but it is something that affects our perception of the treated frequencies.

Depending on the nature of the displacement, we perceive the treated frequencies as distance. Why is this important?

This is what differentiates the tonal characteristics of analogue hardware and digital software EQs.

The analogue EQ unit will exhibit far more musical phase changes than its digital counterpart, and at very low gains, whereas the digital EQ unit will have the advantage of leaving the phase relationships hardly affected, thus allowing for more robust gain changes. They both have their uses.

Tip

Parametric filters are great for more complex filtering jobs and can be used to create real dynamic effects because they can attenuate or boost any range of frequencies.

Tip

Understand frequencies and sound, and you will be in total control.

Compression

The simplest way to describe the function of a compressor is as follows: a compressor makes the quiet bits louder and the loud bits quieter. It acts as an automatic volume control.

In the old days…ah, dem days, we used to adopt a technique called 'gain riding'. Gain was a nice Welsh girl that … no seriously though.

Gain riding: When you had audio passing through the mixer, for example: vocals, we used to pull the volume (gain) fader down when the vocals were being sung too loud, and push it up when the vocals were dropping in level. But this was never too accurate as you had to anticipate when the vocals would rise or drop in gain.

So, enter the compressor. There was much joy to be had. Grapes came out, wanton wenches were brought in, and the odd cow was slaughtered and barbecued there, right in front of the Neve. It was truly a happy time for studio engineers.

By using the compressor, we were able to achieve a far more consistent and stable gain across the audio. By using the threshold level, we were able to control when the compressor would kick into action, and the amount of compression (ratio) to be used on the material. We were also able to set the speed of the compressor kicking in (attack) and how quickly for it to go back to normal (release). Add to that the ability to set the amount of gain reduction, and we had a potent tool.

Today, compressors have become creative tools as well as dynamic controllers, and it is fair to say, at least in the commercial dance markets, that using a compressor is a must.

Unfortunately, the compressor is also being abused. It has become a 'boost' tool as opposed to a dynamic controller. I often see audio data that is so compressed that it breaks down into a square wave.

Compression: hard and soft knee

Let us understand and thus use the compressor for what it should be used for, and to do this, let us take a closer look at its features. Figures 4.5 and 4.6 show what happens when audio is compressed.

Threshold

This is the input level above which compression occurs. Above this level, the output increases at a lesser rate than the corresponding input stage. Set the threshold high to compress only the loudest part of the signal, set it low to compress more of the signal.

Ratio

This is the ratio of the change in input level to the change in output level. For example, a 2:1 ratio means that for every 2dB change in input level, the output changes 1dB.

A 'soft-knee' characteristic is a low compression ratio for low-level signals and a high ratio for high-level signals. With infinite setting, the output stays the same no matter how much you increase the input.

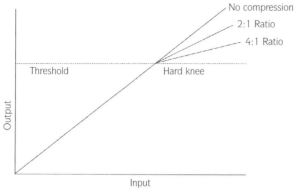

Figure 4.5
Hard knee compression

Figure 4.6
Soft knee compression

Attack

This is how fast the compressor reduces the gain when a signal is input. Basically, the time it takes to kick in. Longer attack times mean that more of the signal goes through, before it starts to get compressed.

Release

This is how fast the compressor returns to neutral, or how fast the gain returns to normal. Short release times give the famous 'pumping' or 'breathing' sound, and are good for following rapid gain changes. Long release times sound more natural and don't interfere with the sound's harmonics.

Gain reduction

This is the number of dB that the gain is reduced by the compressor, and varies with the input level. This is displayed on the meter.

Side chain

Mainly available on hardware compressors, and used for inserting an EQ or filter, or any device, into the signal path, independently of the main input signal, so that the compressor responds only to frequencies boosted by the input device/signal, in this case the EQ.

The EQ does not affect the actual input signal – only the controls of the unit – the controls then adjust the actual main input signal. They can also be used creatively and make for some great effects.

Output control or gain makeup

Because we are squashing peaks in the signal, we are actually reducing the overall peak level, increasing the output level compensates for the volume drop. Turn this level up until the peak levels of the compressed signal match the bypassed signal peaks.

Peak/RMS

RMS stands for Root Mean Square and is a mathematical term for a method of averaging the level of a complex waveform. If your compressor has a Peak/RMS switch, this will determine how the compressor evaluates the incoming sound level and your choice for selection is dependent on the type of material you will be compressing.

The beauty of using RMS is that we, as humans (some of us anyway), tend to use this method for listening. Our ears average out incoming audio, so RMS works in the same way.

But, as stated, the method chosen is dependent on the audio being processed. For short signals, such as drum sounds, Peak will work much better. In Peak mode, the compressor takes action based on the peak level of the input signal, no matter how long or short the sound is. In this instance, using a fast attack time and the Peak setting will afford far better sonic control over the audio than RMS

Knee

Knee refers to the way the compressor reacts when the input level reaches the threshold. A hard-knee compressor brings in all the gain reduction as soon as the signal crosses the threshold.

A soft knee on the other hand brings in the compression more progressively by gradually increasing the compression ratio as the signal level approaches the threshold. Again, the decision in choice is down to the material being processed.

Now let us take a brief look at the different types of compressors.

Stereo/Dual Channel Compressor

If a compressor is to be used on a stereo track, it is important that a stereo compressor or dual channel compressor be used.

Dual channel compressors feature a stereo link switch that effectively sums the two channel levels together and then uses this combined signal to control both channels. In this way, the same gain reduction is applied to both channels at all times.

If the two sides worked independently, then the compressor would sound as if it were shifting from side to side, as audio will vary in loudness from channel to channel.

When linked for stereo operation, both channels of the compressor react to a mix of the sound passing through the two channels so both always react together, regardless of the level balance between the two channels.

Tip

I tend to find that RMS works really well on longer, undulating sounds, like vocals, and Peak works well on short sounds, like percussion.

Multiband Compressor

These divide the incoming audio signal into multiple bands, with each band being compressed independently from the other.

The beauty of this is that with full band compressors, that we have been discussing till now, the whole signal is treated, so when a peak is detected, the whole signal is compressed and so other frequencies are also subject to compression.

Multiband compression only compresses the frequency bands chosen, so a more fluid and less abrupt result is gained. Instead of having one peak trigger the compressor into compressing the entire signal, the multiband allows for individual bands to be compressed.

On some compressors, you even have the option of selecting bands that will not undergo any treatment. After passing through the filters, each frequency band is fed into its own compressor, after which the signals are recombined at the output.

Another feature of the multiband compressor is that you are offered crossover points. This is crucial, as you are given control over where to place the frequency bands. Setting these crossover points is the heart of the compressor and crucial in processing the right frequency spectrum with the right settings.

For example: if you are treating the vocals in the mid range but put your low end crossover too far into the middle range, then the low end compression settings will also affect the mid range vocals.

Limiter

A limiter keeps signal peaks from exceeding a pre determined level. While a compressor reduces the overall dynamic range, a limiter affects only the highest peaks. Limiters have very fast attack times, very high compression ratios and a high threshold. The 'classic' definition is that a limiter 'flattens' all peaks above a certain level, but leaves lower-level sounds intact.

I think this is enough as far as compressors are concerned, until we come to practical uses, and it is then that we will discuss Upward Compression, Parallel Compression and Noise.

For now, we have covered, albeit briefly, the two most important dynamics and the most frequently used effects. In the virtual world, these distinct tools start to merge and become more blurry to explain.

Software is so laden with features that it is not uncommon to find an effect incorporated within a dynamic plug-in, and vice versa. In fact, we now have software plug-in compressors that also house effects and noise elimination characteristics, along with a host of other features that would normally be adorned in separate hardware units.

Tip

In essence, a multi-band compressor comprises a set of filters that splits the audio signal into two or more frequency bands.

Tip

The main advantage of multi-band compression is that a loud event in one frequency band won't trigger gain reduction in the other bands.

Tip

You can turn your compressor into a limiter by using a very high threshold and ratio.

Tip

The world is changing, and so must our thinking and approach. But it is fair to say that good old fashioned practices still win the day as far as mixing and production goes.

Headphones and speakers

So, we have now arrived to the point of no return. We must mix! But soon ... soon.

Before we plunge into that world which can only be equated as 'madness', I must impart to you a few words of wisdom, wisdom that the great Siph Lord LET (Low End Theory) passed down to me when I was but a small Padewan.

Just prior to an 'incident' that involved a sabre or two, and some back stabbing, he uttered the words 'Monitor with both speakers and cans'. (Cans, as you know, is a term meaning headphones.)

All jokes aside, this is actually very good advice and one that I am glad to share with you. Why is the advice so good? It takes care of the two most obvious, and yet mostly ignored, problems encountered when mixing:

- Stereo imaging
- Noise

Stereo imaging

Stereo imaging is what we have been preparing for with all our intricate setting up and calibrating procedures. It is all about getting the best stereo image from all the components of the mix, the important balance of all the audio in the mix and where all the individual instruments and voices sit in the mix, all amassed together to form one single stereo mix.

Stereo imaging also takes into account the depth of the mix, the width and the overall clarity of all the components that go to form the mix.

Height within a mix can be attained by comb filtering but that is not a subject I want to get into now as we are dealing with a stereo master and not surround of any sort.

Although stereo imaging is the stereo field representation of the mix as a Left/Right output, it goes far beyond that, entailing processes involved at attaining the perfect stereo image, because within this field there are many components that must be placed correctly in order to accentuate position.

Did that confuse you? Ok, let me put it this way: to attain a perfect stereo image, you need to take into account the overall placement of the sounds within the mix and how they interact with each other. There, you can't get an easier explanation than that.

A simple example of how this works is as follows:

Info

Cans, as you know, is a term meaning headphones.

Tip

Although stereo imaging is the stereo field representation of the mix as a left/right output, it goes far beyond that, entailing processes involved in attaining the perfect stereo image, because within this field there are many components that must be placed correctly in order to accentuate position.

- Take a kick and a snare and play them as a simple 4/4 pattern with both sounds central (panned middle).
- Now, add a hihat pattern into the beat and pan this off centre to the right.
- Now, listen to the beat and it will sound off-axis, not centred but biased to the right field.

All it took was one sound that gave the perception of imbalance. To then further explore this method:

- Add a cabasa pattern to the beat and pan it off centre to the left.
- Now, listen to the beat and it will sound more balanced.

Gain boosting and gain reduction

This is how you build balance in the stereo field. Let's not stop there. Let's go even further with this particular example.

- Raise the gain (volume) of the hihats
- The beat sounds off-axis again and biased to the right.

This teaches us that volume has a strong and direct relationship with how we perceive placement of sound in a stereo field. The more volume a particular sound has in relation to other sounds, the more accentuated it will be in the stereo field, and thus make the listener pick out the louder sound in the field and therefore imbalance the mix.

This also works in our favour, particularly where vocals are involved, as we can accentuate a centrally panned vocal and therefore make the listener pay attention to the vocals, and the surrounding sounds are there to fill the field and yet keep the listener focused on the vocals.

Let's go all the way, now that we have come this far. By boosting the frequencies of a sound (EQ), we are in effect accentuating it in the mix and it will stand out in the field, same as volume, because boosting certain frequencies is the same as raising the volume of the frequencies.

Both the above can be achieved in reverse, by reducing the volume of a sound, or reducing certain frequencies of a sound; we in effect raise the presence of the sounds around the affected sound.

A better way of explaining this is to take the example of the vocals and reduce the gain of the vocals in the mix. All of a sudden the sounds around the vocals sound louder. I think you are starting to get the idea now.

You do not always need to boost frequencies to attain the perception of volume or placement; you can achieve this by simple gain reduction techniques of the surrounding material.

We will attack this subject with serious hands on mangling of frequencies when we come to actually mix a song. Aren't you overwhelmed with utter excitement? Mmm ... I thought so.

It doesn't end there either.

Tip

You do not always need to boost frequencies to attain the perception of volume or placement; you can achieve this by simply reducing the gain of the surrounding material.

Tip

Remember, it is about perception.

Filtering

Filtering also has the same effect as frequency reduction or boosting. By filtering out low frequencies, the mid and high frequencies sound more pronounced, and vice versa. Remember, it is about perception.

This filtering technique can work wonders in a mix.

- Filtering certain low end frequencies from the bass sound can give more emphasis to the kick sound, or vice versa.
- Filtering the low end of en entire mix can give more emphasis to the mid and high ends of the mix.
- Filtering the high end off hihats can give more warmth to the drum beat.
- Layering the lead vocal and filtering the low end off one layer can give a rounded and more emphasized vocal line and fill the mix a little more.

This goes on and on. You will find that filtering can have either subtle or dramatic consequences on a sound or a mix. Use it wisely. We will come to this later, and in practice.

Mono sounds

Let's now take a look at mono sounds. Mono sounds move in totality when panned in a mix. That means that they are far more pronounced when moved along the pan axis than stereo sounds.

In reality, what happens to a stereo sound when it is panned is that one channel is boosted, as opposed to both, and if you wanted to achieve total control over both channels in the stereo field, you would need to use two channels to control both sides of the field. This is completely different to using a stereo sound on one channel in a mixer.

The best way to explain this is by example. Try moving a bass sound that is in mono across the pan axis and do the same with a bass sound that is in stereo and on one channel in the mixer and listen to the difference. It can be quite pronounced depending on the sound used.

Stereo sounds are already panned wide, so trying to move a stereo sound moves the entire width of the stereo field. This limits it in both localization of placement (as it covers a wider area) and in definition (as it is spread across a wider area).

However, where stereo sounds rule is in the space they occupy and this gives the sound a huge presence. A piano sound in stereo will sound much fuller and spacious than in mono, whereas a kick drum will sound more pronounced in mono.

Personally, I like to start by mixing all my sounds in mono and then worrying about what needs to end up as stereo. This gives me far better placement control. We will come to this later. I have devoted a whole chapter (Chapter 7) to the subject of Mixing for Stereo. For now, all I am concerned with is using headphones to ascertain certain qualities within a mix and how these can be missed when monitoring on speakers.

Monitoring on speakers will afford you a proper stereo image as opposed to working with headphones. Headphones will, however, excel in providing you with a true and accurate breakdown of sound placement.

Tip

Filtering the low end of en entire mix can give more emphasis to the mid and high ends of the mix.

Info

In reality, what happens to a stereo sound when it is panned is that one channel is boosted, as opposed to both.

Tip

Experiment and follow your ears.

Info

Monitoring on speakers will afford you a proper stereo image as opposed to working with headphones. Headphones will, however, excel in providing you with a true and accurate breakdown of sound placement.

Noise

You would be surprised at how many producers ignore this in the whole mass of audio that they are dealing with.

It is so easy to *not* hear noise when you are past the start of a track with all the components playing their bits. This is where headphones come into their own league. You hear amazing detail with headphones and it is this detail that exposes any anomalies in the mix.

Noise comes in many formats

Clicks, hiss, low level rumble, pops, vocal sibilance etc should all be treated as noise. Some would regard sibilance or popping of ppp, bbb or ttt whilst singing as 'singing'. I call it noise because it needs to be treated and removed.

First off I always leave a few seconds of lead-in to the song, where no instruments are playing and all you are hearing is the sound card and the gain settings of the mixer (hardware or virtual). Bear in mind effects and dynamics have inherent noise too and this can only be heard in isolation or during the lead-in. The lead-in will reveal any hums, hisses or rumbles. Because, once the music starts, they will be masked by the overlying sounds.

It is also good practice to leave a few seconds of lead-out at the end of the mix to further check and analyze any anomalies that might have crept in unnoticed. It is at this point that you can check list the components that might cause any of these anomalies.

Tip

Headphones can isolate noise because the sound is not washed out and saturated into the surrounding environment (speakers), but kept intact within the headphone's sound field.

Tip

The lead-in will reveal any hums, hisses or rumbles. Because, once the music starts, they will be masked by the overlying sounds.

Info

Personally, I run a noise filter across the main stereo outs of my mixer, or master sub outs, prior to the sound card's inputs, in order to remove any hiss or similar from the mix prior to the record master stage. For this, I use a Drawmer DF330. Some producers use noise gates across the mixer's channels (if they have them) or across the main outs, much as I do.

In a virtual domain and with a sound card, this particular problem is lessened to the point of negligence.

- Low level hum or rumble can be filtered out using a notch filter, band pass or a high pass filter. EQ can also help, but you can generally find the cause of low level hum to be an amp of some sort, monitor interference, earth loops etc.

Info

We use headphones in tandem with speakers, in order to isolate noise and sound placement in a mix (headphones) and to reveal the integrity and clarity of the stereo field (speakers).

- Isolate and eradicate these prior to any recording or mixing. Try not to eradicate by using dynamics as this just adds another generation of processing, and therefore noise, but try to find the actual cause of the hum etc. and fix it.
- Pops can be eradicated by using pop shields during vocal takes and sibilance can be treated with de-essers.

I do not want to go into this area in great depth as this is more to do with the recording process and this book is focused on mixing.

Mixing to stereo

I think it imperative to explain what it is we do when mixing to a stereo master. You have to remember that when you are listening to a band or an orchestra performing on stage, you are listening to the environment as much as the individual sounds.

The environment of the venue will produce natural reverberation. This reverberation will undoubtedly mask most of the acoustic information you need in order to determine the positions of the sound sources. You will be able to ballpark the position of a sound but with little accuracy. This can be said of almost all naturally reverberated sounds. It is impossible to exactly pinpoint the position of the source signal, so we approximate.

In a studio, that thinking changes, as we have detailed control over the placement of a sound, the amount of gain of that sound, the amount, and type, of reverberation used and so on. We are, in effect, trying to recreate the natural space needed for the mix with technical means.

However, the idea of mixing for natural space has now gone well beyond that premise, and we now mix artistically, and it is this technical ability that has allowed us to define certain genres and feels.

The tools we have at our disposal makes for infinite variations of a mix. This can be overwhelming at first, but once the technical side has been mastered, the results can be extremely fruitful.

The technicalities and aesthetic decisions undertaken to complete the mix are then honed and resulted to one single stereo master. This single file will be the representation of the entire mix process. It is your duty to faithfully and artistically master all the tools and processes needed to achieve as close to a perfect mix as possible. It is this mix that the listener listens to, not the tales of how you achieved it. Those tales are reserved for tech talks at the local bar.

You might also feel the need to debate with me the word 'perfect' and how nothing can be perfect. I am afraid that as far as the technical aspects of mixing go, there are certain criteria that must be met. This in no way defines perfection, but does define the technical merit of the mix.

We are not talking about artistic perfection, as this does not exist, but that of technical merit. This is not a grey area, so please don't think it is.

Everything prior to this chapter has been to prepare you and your environment for the mix process. For without proper calibration and preparation, you will be working blind and the road to a good mix will be an alley that leads nowhere.

Tip

Do not take shortcuts. This is not an exam or a quick fix scenario.

Each morsel of information that you acquire will compound your abilities. Each procedure you go through will discipline you to the point where these boring procedures become second nature to you. Everything helps. Ignore nothing.

For the purposes of this book, I have chosen to mix in the virtual domain (computer), as this is what most home studios and semi pro studios do. A combination of both would be far better in terms of attaining top quality results, and I am sure this is what you will strive to achieve. Almost all commercial studios adopt a hybrid system of hardware and software.

The mix

For this book I have chosen a mix contract that has come my way from G.A.M. Productions. The purpose of this contract is to produce and master the content. However, for the purposes of this tutorial, I am only going to mix the content and maybe add to it musically.

The tracks are all in extremely raw form, and I have deliberately left in all the recording errors that came with the contract. These errors are not the fault of G.A.M, but of the studio that recorded them. I will not name the studio or engineers involved. However, the errors are glaringly obvious and I am glad that they exist as it will help you to understand what needs to be done to correct them.

Info

All audio examples contained within this book are available for download at the following url:

http://www.samplecraze.com/sound-mixing/

It is important to download and audition these audio files in the order that they appear in within this book.

Tip

To be able to truthfully mix any material, you need to have the recordings in optimum condition.

When I receive contracts of this nature, the recordings usually consist of very few effects or dynamics. I also receive the sessions' mixes so that I have a guide for the effects and dynamics used, in the event that I need them. What we are concerned with is the raw recorded data and that's pretty much it.

To be able to truthfully mix any material, you need to have the recordings in optimum quality condition. If the recordings suffer from any anomalies, be they noise or gain issues, then you can choose to reject them or to correct them as part of the agreed contract.

Tip

Make sure you have the session mixes, session notes and any other relevant information that will help you in providing a good mix in the agreed timeline.

Personally, I always inform the client of any anomalies that exist in the mix as these will take time to correct and some cannot even be corrected. So, make sure the material you are going to mix is presented in as near perfect condition as possible, prior to you commencing the mix process.

Before commencing the mix process, think through the layout, and plan your process out thoroughly. I will explain this in detail in the next chapter.

Creating the mix

As we are dealing with the virtual domain, I will be using Cubase SX 3 for the mixing process. I will also be using additional plug-ins for the effects and dynamics.

Import the audio tracks

The first stage of the mixing process is to import all the audio tracks into mono channels in the sequencer. I always start with mono channels for the reasons I outlined earlier.

I use the phrase 'channel' for' track' as we will be dealing with channels in the mixer section which is directly relevant to what is both in the arrange window and in the mixer window.

Sound stage refers to the performance stage and where the instruments/performers are placed. So, in a sound stage scenario, the singer would probably be placed right bang in the middle (centre stage) and up front, assuming he isn't on one of his walkabouts.

By the same thinking, the drummer would be central but behind the band. I have heard this is because drummers are particularly ugly and so always demoted out of the public's view ... hahahahahahah!

Back to the mix. I will load (if the song has been provided in Cubase format), or import (if all I have are just the audio tracks) into Cubase, selecting mono channels for all the audio tracks. I always try to section the relevant audio files together. As you can see from Figure 8.1, I have imported all the drum audio files into a sensible order and grouped them together.

I also try to group the necessary categories/types of sounds together. This makes for easy navigation and editing. By keeping all the hihat channels together I can always find the necessary channel in an instant as I know that all the hihats are grouped together in a section of the mixer.

The same is true for all the other sounds. I will keep all lead vocal lines together, kick sounds together, backing vocals together etc. This not only affords me easy navigation, and is visually clean and well laid out, but it also allows me to make quick adjustments to a sound whilst comparing it to another respective sound, e.g: if I am applying EQ to a kick sound, it helps tremendously if the next kick sound (assuming I am using more than one kick sound) is next to the one I am editing. This way, I can go to one channel and then the next and edit them side by side. This saves time and makes the editing process much simpler. Imagine having to tweak a kick sound then having

Tip

I can perform a better sound-field (sound stage) mix using mono channels than stereo channels.

Info

I always try to section the relevant audio files together.

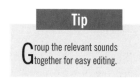

Tip

Group the relevant sounds together for easy editing.

Figure 8.1
Importing drum channels

to find the next kick sound, halfway down the mixer channels, and then editing that and then coming back and … well, you get the picture.

So, simply select a new song/mix or whatever it is called in your sequencer, and then create audio mono channels. You can do this in one hit if you know how many channels you will need, or, as I do, create the channels as I go along importing audio files. This leaves me scope to make any parameter settings I see fit as I am importing.

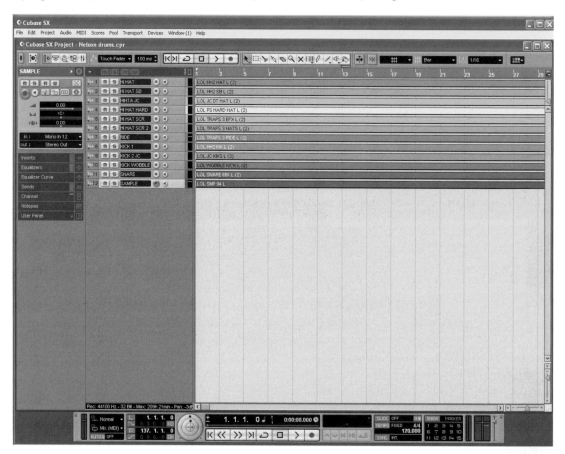

As you can see from Figure 8.1, I have all the hihats and ride grouped first, then the kicks, snare and, finally, the sample.

Also note how I have staged the Cubase layout. I have made sure that I am using the full width of the main (arrange) pane, and have left enough room to import all the other audio files, notably the vocals. I have also kept the transport in view, but right at the bottom of the pane so as not to get in my way.

I generally use shortcut key commands to access all the necessary panes and editing tools. But for the purposes of this tutorial, I will use the transport and mouse to make it easier for you to follow.

So, we now have all our percussive elements imported and grouped together. Another reason why I like working this way is that if at any point, as we might do later, I want to add another channel of audio or MIDI music; I can simply group it with the relevant sound category, as I have done above with the drum sounds.

Label channels clearly

I always clearly label channels in capitals so that I do not have to screw up my eyes just to read what is where. This system of grouping is a great way to work and keeps everything tidy and remarkably easy when it comes to editing. Being able to add audio or MIDI channels to the necessary section is another time saving and sensible move.

Next, I start to import all the vocal audio files into the main arrangement, again keeping in line with the methodology. Let us first create another audio channel so we can import the audio files. As Figure 8.2 shows, it is dead easy to create new tracks/channels in Cubase. I generally create the channels one at a time, as I stated earlier.

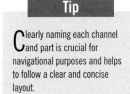

Tip

Be clear and sensible in both naming and grouping channels. Make this a habit.

Tip

Clearly naming each channel and part is crucial for navigational purposes and helps to follow a clear and concise layout.

Figure 8.2
Creating new audio channels

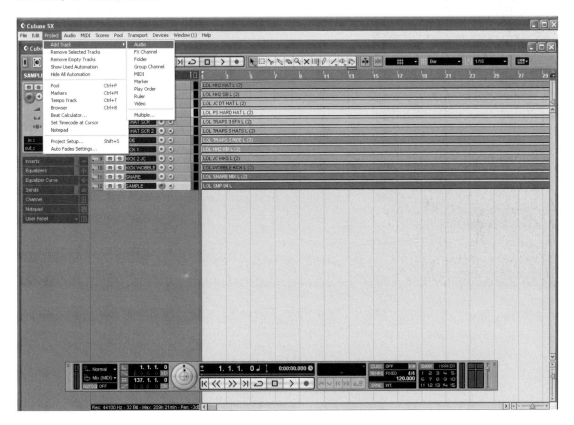

As you can see from Figure 8.3, I have kept the vocals sensibly grouped also. I try to keep the lead vocals together, the backing vocals together and the spit (rap) together. You can take this a stage further and group the female and male vocals in their own respective groups. In this mix, there are no female vocals to consider, but it is best to mention this now as your mix might.

Figure 8.3
Import the vocals – grouping them
logically

I have also selected different colours for the channels as this is the quickest way to locate a channel in the mixer window. I keep the vocal channels in one colour, so as not to confuse them with any of the instrument channels. However, this is all about personal preference. You could leave all the channels at default color if that is how you work.

It is important to note, at this juncture, that you do not need to do anything apart from importing files and sensibly grouping them together. After this process is over, we will start to process a basic gain mix.

Create an order of events

Before we start our mix, let us create an order of events. I generally stick to the same sequence of processes.

- I create the arrangement and group and name all the files/channels, as we have done above.
- I will then check each and every file for noise, distortion etc.
- I create a level and pan mix.
- This is the stage that dynamics and effects come into play.
- I add to the track/song musically and maybe rearrange as well.
- I perform another level and pan mix and add any additional effects and/or dynamics

That is pretty much it.

Check the files for noise

Let us now check the files for noise etc. The audio example in Figure 8.4 clearly shows the noise inherent in this file. I have taken care to only upload a small portion of this audio file so as not to hog the bandwidth and enclose a huge file. However, the clip is long enough for you to appreciate what I am pointing out.

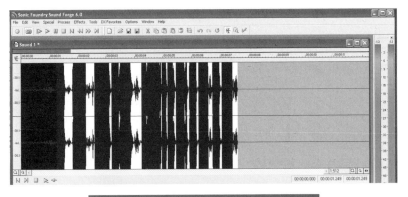

Figure 8.4
Noise present in the sound file.

Sound file

Lead vocal bleed

Info

All audio examples contained within this book are available for download at the following url:

http://www.samplecraze.com/sound-mixing/

It is important to download and audition these audio files in the order that they appear in within this book.

Figure 8.5 shows both the channel noise in the file in Cubase, and a zoomed image of the highlighted noise in Sound Forge. It is clear that the

Figure 8.5
Lead vocal bleed audio example

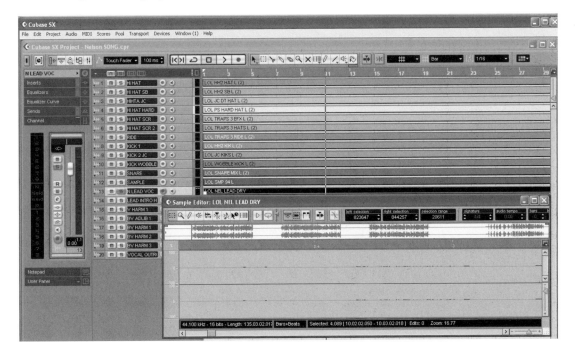

noise element in the lead vocal is headphone bleed. This happens when the foldback (headphone setup to singer) has not been prepared with care.

We create a foldback situation and send the instrumental, and sometimes the backing vocal mix with it, to the singer's headphones so the singer can hear what he/she is singing to and can also hear his/her voice in the overall mix.

In the event that the headphone gain is too loud, or the headphones are open backed (as opposed to closed back headphones), the music being sent to the singer's headphones will 'bleed' into the microphone and will get recorded along with the singer's vocals. This is so common and so annoying, but can be avoided with easy and sensible planning.

The height of the audio peaks above is apparent because I have expanded the height using the zoom tool, not because they are compressed or peaking too loud.

Removing the noise

There are a few ways of dealing with correcting this problem.

- You can be meticulous and lower the gain of each and every segment of bleed in the whole lead vocal file by using the appropriate tool in your audio editor.
- You can run a noise gate across the whole channel and gate out the bleed.
- You could use EQ or filtering to remove, or reduce, the bleed.

The easiest, and most widely used, of all the techniques available for correcting a file of this nature is to use a noise gate across the channel. Basically it does what it sounds like. It acts as a gate and opens when a threshold is reached and then closes depending on how fast a release you set, basically acting as an on-off switch.

It reduces gain when the input level falls below the set threshold, that is, when an instrument or audio stops playing, or reaches a gap where the level drops, the noise gate kicks in and reduces the volume of the file. The noise gate is used precisely for this type of situation, so why not use it here?

The noise gate is used as an insert on a mixer. In the case of the virtual mixer, the noise gate is selected and used much as any other vst effect.

For your learning benefit, I am going to show you how to gate the bleed from the file in two ways, and discuss a third.

The first (Example 1) will entail running a noise gate across the audio file of the lead vocal in an audio editor. I use Sound Forge so that is what I am going to use for the examples in this book.

The second (Example 2) method is the one we discussed above; running a noise gate across the lead vocal channel as a VST effect.

Example 1

As you can see from Figure 8.6, I am selecting the noise gate effect from the 'effect' drop down menu in Sound Forge.

Tip

A noise gate is a great dynamic.

Info

Another useful feature of a noise gate is the side-chain input (key input), where an external signal controls the opening and closing of the gate. This makes it a great musical tool. Key inputting a hi hat pattern to trigger the gate while playing a whooshing pad sound, gives the effect of the pad sound being chopped, much like a Trance gate. Is that cool, or is that cool?

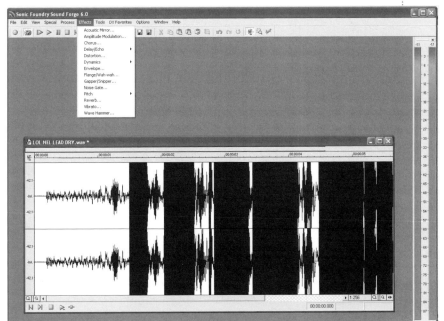

Figure 8.6
Select the noise gate 'effect' from the drop down menu.

After selecting the noise gate as the effect to be used, and using its preset drop down menu, I can either select a predefined preset for the gate or edit my own from the parameters on offer, Figure 8.7.

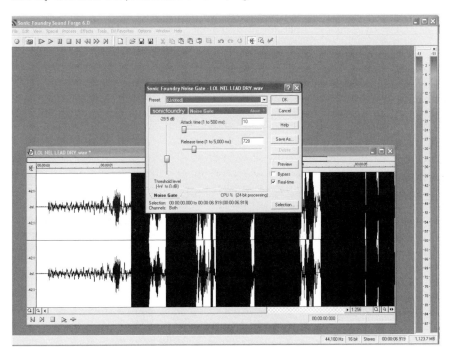

Figure 8.7
Select a predefined preset for the gate or edit one from the parameters on offer

Figure 8.8
Waveform after gate
effect has been applied

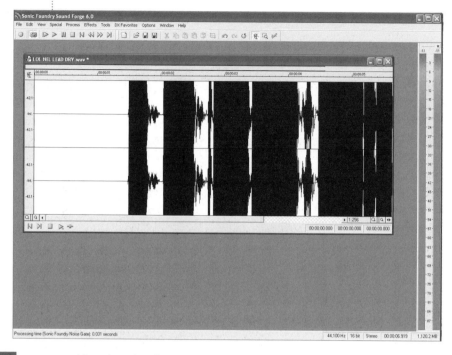

After changing the parameter settings and processing the waveform, I get
Figure 8.8.

The crucial part of this process is to make sure you do not gate the singing
itself or any part of the harmonics that are there as part of the way the singer
sings. Start with very low and weak settings, and work up from there.

Go through the entire audio file to make sure the gate is not gating out
the quieter parts of the vocal file. Pay particular attention to how words start
and how they tail off.

As you can see and hear from the example above, the bleed has now completely gone. A good way of finding out if all the noise etc has been removed
is to actually enlarge (zoom) the file and look for any slight peaks where there
are no sung parts.

Example 2

The process is exactly the same as working in an audio editor. I sometimes
suggest that all files be edited outside of the sequencer first and then imported back in once the editing is complete. This saves having to edit within the
sequencer and, more importantly, it saves on CPU power as you do not have
to have multiple instances of gate vsts open on varying channels.

Figure 8.9 shows the mixer window, the audio channel window where you
select effects etc, and the gate effect I have chosen from the drop down menu.

A few things to note are; the mixer window shows me the selected and
active lead vocal channel which I have soloed so I can hear it in isolation and
the metering shows you which channel it is, the audio channel window where
the lead vocal resides in is also showing and it shows that I have chosen
'Dynamics' as the effect for that particular channel, and finally, the effect
itself is showing with all its parameter settings.

Follow the same procedure as you would if you were editing the file in the audio editor. Gate the whole file and play the soloed channel, checking for any anomalies. If you need to be very precise, then open the audio file in the editor and check to make sure everything is fine.

Figure 8.9
The mixer window, the audio channel window where you select effects etc, and the gate effect I have chosen from the drop down menu.

Example 3
Using EQ or filters to correct the bleed problem is not one that I recommend as the bleed itself will have varying frequencies, so using any banded EQ will not be too accurate unless you select a wide band, and when you do that you could affect frequencies that are inherent within the vocals. Using filters throws up similar problems.

To effectively use a filter you need to ascertain the exact frequency band that needs filtering, otherwise you have the same problems as using EQ.

I could actually spend pages describing how to use EQ and filters to eradicate bleed, but that would be a waste of space. I would rather reserve these particular tools for the mixing process itself instead of corrective procedures that would not be entirely successful.

Of course you can use these tools for corrective procedures, but not in this instance as the frequencies that we need to abate will be shared with the vocal's frequencies.

Tip

The noise gate is an old school weapon, used by many engineers and as far back as mixers have existed, well almost.

Within the files that have been sent to me for the mix, there exist a few files that have already been gated at the recording stage. This is an old and tried practice and works extremely well if you decide you need to record vocals and there is noise in the signal. This noise could be the mix knocking about, general hiss, 'bleeding' etc. You set up the noise gate as an insert on the microphone channel, and set the threshold so that the noise is abated and then record the vocals.

As with the examples above, let your ears decide what the best setting for the vocals is. I cannot give you magic settings as each situation has its own unique properties dependent on the room used, the mic used and so on.

Be aware that the noise gate is not demoted to just removing bleed but is used for a number of tasks. Removing any anomaly that relies on gain control is an area that the gate excels in. If the problem is consistent in gain, then the gate can work wonders.

There is, of course, the musical aspect of using a gate, as mentioned earlier. So, you really do have a well defined and general tool in the toolbox. Use it!

At this point, I do not want use any EQ or compression. All I am after is clean files, with proper gain settings and panned and placed in the stereo field. You can suffer as much from too narrow a field as too wide a field. So, it always makes sense to work off what we call the quarter to 3 (or 9 and 3), these being pan positions of the mixer's pan knobs.

Tip

A common mistake that most people make is to assume that the more extreme you push that pan dial, the better the stereo spread. This is in fact incorrect.

If you go beyond these values, you are, in effect, stretching the extremes of the stereo field. Although the pans are still going left and right, the extent to which the extremes have been pushed often stretch the stereo field too far.

In certain instances this can be a good idea but I prefer, certainly at this stage of the mix process, to work off smaller values and then to reconsider the stereo field in its entirety when the time comes for the final mix. It is always better to display 'space' in your mixes than coloured reverb effects. Of course, there are times when the coloured reverb effect is exactly what you might need on a certain instrument, but for a good mix, space is what you should be striving to attain.

Tip

You can attain a wide and natural stereo spread by clever use of reverbs.

A common mistake that most people make is to assume that the more extreme you push that pan dial, the better the stereo spread. This is in fact incorrect. You can attain a wide and natural stereo spread by clever use of reverbs.

The level and pan mix

So, now we need to adjust all the gains for all the channels, and set basic pan positions so we have a better idea of what needs adjusting. It is at this time that I make decisions about which effects and dynamics to use.

By using effects I am able to create space and colour. By using dynamics I am able to emphasize a sound in the stereo field and to further define it so it can stand out or blend in with the rest of the mix.

The trick with gain setting is to keep the levels a few dB below peak (0). I tend to work off -6 dB, and sometimes more if I know I will be using a compressor on the channel, and even more if I know I am going to supplement the channel compressor with a main stereo mix compressor.

This allows me the leverage within headroom for any dynamic processing. Compressors and EQ will invariably boost the signal, unless you are using the compressor for dynamic control as opposed to boosting. A good mix can be compression free if you have good dynamic movement, because it is the dynamic movement that gives the perception of gain. We touched on this earlier.

I can use automation to control gains, as opposed to using compression for gain control, but this is a topic best left for later when we are fine tweaking the overall mix.

Levels (gains)

Start off by moving all the channel faders to about halfway so that the metering shows a midway signal level (Figure 9.1).

As you can see, I have moved the main stereo fader to the 0 position. This will give me a proper readout with no clipping as I have already calibrated my signal path. If the signal clips, then I do not need to look beyond the individual channels themselves as the cause of the problem. By sticking with these low to mid values, it is much easier to work out the peaks in each channel.

I usually start by creating overall mid levels for every channel, so that my ears don't burst because of any major peaks in the mix. It also helps my ears to attune themselves gently, as opposed to an aggressive influx of volume.

Once I achieve this very basic level mix, I start to work channel by channel, soloing and listening to each channel right through. This helps me to pick out spikes in the level and to mark, with locators, the areas that will require attention. By setting these markers, I can then name each marker as to what needs doing.

Figure 9.1
Main stereo fader set to the 0 position.

An example of this would be to mark in a locator when a spike is found, and name it for compression or a gain reduction of some sort. I then continue through the whole channel, creating markers and naming them, for different tasks.

You could also use the audio editor in your sequencer and process the spikes accordingly by highlighting the spiked area and using one of the tools within the software.

However, in practice, I usually have a good idea as to what I will need and where I will need it. If the audio has been recorded properly, I will not need to do too much corrective processing, but if there are spikes and level drops in the audio, then I will need to mark the affected areas and use whatever means I find suitable to correct the flaws.

The solo function on a mixer, hardware or virtual, is your best friend when it comes to mixing. Not only can you listen to a specific track/channel in isolation but you can isolate more than one track/channel at a time. This makes for a useful way of comparing one track with another, or, as an example, to solo all the drum tracks/channels and work on them separately to the rest of the mix. Following on from this example, you can then bring in instruments one at a time. Bass would be next and by soloing the drum parts and the bass channel, you can listen for any frequency clashes etc.

Tip

Add the solo button to your arsenal of special producer's weapons.

Pans

There are a few basic pointers you can follow when panning certain sounds. The most important thing to bear in mind here is that low frequency sounds like bass guitars, bass synthesizers and kick drums work best when panned to the centre. This is due to the fact that they contain most of the energy within a mix, so it is best to share the load of reproducing them equally across both speakers so that there is balance when listening.

Energy must always be kept central as any bias will be exposed mercilessly. Using any form of stereo widening tools on bass sounds, or trying to stretch the bass to occupy the stereo field, is not a good idea. Sometimes, as an effect, it can work, but stretching bass sounds always imbalances the mix and plays havoc with the other sounds in the field.

Panning synthetic sounds

Earlier we discussed the pan positioning of certain sounds and how to use the sound stage as a guide to where certain instruments can be placed. What we did not touch on is how to pan synthetic sounds.

It is easy using a sound stage as a guide on placing orchestral, or acoustic bands, sounds in the stereo field, as we can look at where the musicians are placed within the orchestra/band, but trying to work out where certain synthetic sounds sit in a mix requires that we use our ears and mind to best determine what are the most important sounds in the mix. These sounds take priority and must then share a dominant space in the mix or are better emphasized by other sounds. A good example of this would be to use the hook and pan it central in the mix.

Panning the hook

If the vocals completely occupy the centre stage of the mix, then consider how and where the hook should be presented.

Panning the hook just off centre can work well, but panning it extreme will be poor as the hook is crucial to the mix, much the same as the vocals, so any bias must be qualified. The hook is usually repeated, and in Hip Hop, pretty much continually. So, having the hook sitting hard right or left will completely imbalance the mix and irritate the listener.

Panning synthetic sounds is more about 'filling' the mix. Think of the mix as layers of audio with emphasis on vocals, drums and hooks occupying the most dominant pan areas. Now, build around these components with well balanced and separated sounds. Take particular note of the types of frequencies you are dealing with.

Panning pads

Layering and panning pads are areas that people seem to have issues with.

Think of the frequency content of the pad. If it exhibits low frequencies, then keep the pad sound central. But be aware that you will also have to share frequencies with the bass sound and the kick drum, so make sure not to clutter the frequencies.

If you feel there is too much low-end to the mix, then use EQ or filtering to separate the bass and pad.

> **Tip**
>
> Low frequency sounds like bass guitars, bass synthesizers and kick drums work best when panned to the centre,

> **Tip**
>
> Using any form of stereo widening tools on bass sounds, or trying to stretch the bass to occupy the stereo field, is not a good idea.

> **Tip**
>
> Be sensible when panning hooks. If the hook cannot sit in the centre, then find somewhere sensible for it to reside, making sure you are not too far away from the centre.

> **Tip**
>
> Always think of the overall balance of the mix. Never have bias to either side of the field as this can make for poor listening experiences.

If the pad exhibits higher frequencies, then consider placing them slightly off centre, but again take into account the overall gain of the pad sound as high frequency sounds can dominate a mix as easily as low frequency sounds.

Invariably, the problem with pad sounds is that they are always programmed 'big' and wide, usually being in stereo. Additionally, they can be 'evolving', modulating and moving across the stereo field. So, be very careful when dealing with sounds of this nature.

I tend to 'strip' pad sounds down from all modulation programming that involves such heavy movement across the stereo field, so as to leave a much more neutrally panned sound to deal with.

Always try to cover as much of the frequency spectrum as possible when mixing, even if you only have a few instrument sounds and sparse vocals to play with. In situations such as this, try to spread your sounds across the frequency spectrum, filling up the spaces between each other so that the mix sounds fuller and more spread.

Panning these sounds can also make a huge difference to the way the listener perceives separation. You could pan low end sounds both central and opposite to each other in the stereo field. What you mustn't do is pan a single low end, such as the sounds described earlier, sound anywhere but central. Of course there are exceptions to the low frequency sound being panned elsewhere, but these usually involve orchestral sounds, gongs and the like or low end percussive sounds. Trust me, it can be noticed immediately.

Of course, there are times when the 'sparse' effect is required, but you still need to consider the frequency spaces that these sounds occupy. There is no point in using EQ or filters to narrow the frequency spectrum of each sound and then trying to mix them all together. It is better to allow the frequency of one sound to end as near to the start frequency of the next sound. For example: a bass sound could be thick and deep and dominate the low end. With that in mind, your next sound, let's say a pad sound, could work really well if it takes off where the bass frequency tops-out. This pad sound could then fill the next frequency band until the next sound starts.

This is a tried and trusted method, but, as always, let your ears define what should take place in the mix. However, be aware that mixing frequencies is as important as placing the same frequencies in the stereo field.

Panning drums

Panning where drums are concerned is also crucial. People tend to think that so long as the kick is central and the snare is close to centre, then the hihats and percussive sounds can go anywhere. This is not true. You must treat the drums exactly the same as treating any other sound.

- I always keep my kicks and snares dead central.
- I will sometimes vary the pan of the secondary fill snare but only very slightly.
- I keep hihats within the 9 and 3 limits and rarely let them sway from this.

For certain very synthetic drum sounds, you might want to vary the percussive elements for effect, but you must keep the kick central, particularly for Dance based music and Hip Hop.

Panning vocals

Panning for vocals is probably the most important aspect of any mix. It is generally understood, and practised, that the lead vocals stay dead centre and backing vocals and harmonies can fall on either side of the stereo field. This is okay as long as there is balance on both sides of the field.

I tend to use a lot of tricks when it comes to vocal panning.

- I sometimes create copies of the lead vocals and pan them slightly off centre and this thickens and adds width to the lead vocal.
- With harmonies, I tend to listen to the overall mix and use the sounds in the mix as pointers to where the harmonies should sit.
- If I am using a mid end vocal harmony and there is a strong and dominant mid range sound on the left, off centre, then I will make sure they do not occupy the same space as each other. As a guide, I tend to place them between the 9 and 3 limits and more often than not at the 11 and 1 spots.

Backing vocals are a different kettle of fish as they need to support the lead vocals with backbone, so keeping these close to centre but with copies panned further out works a treat.

The chorus is crucial and makes the song, keep these central. You can work copies off centre, but the main chorus must sit central as the lead vocal does. I will use examples of the above in a minute so you can understand the practice behind the thinking.

Always consider the frequencies of the sounds you are using, whether percussive or otherwise.

Check the sound file

Okay, so let us now conclude the level and pan mix. As you can see from Figure 9.2, I have stuck to sensible pan positions for all the sounds, including the vocals. I have not panned anything too extreme and have taken note of all the levels.

As you can hear from the sound file, I have kept the vocals in the 3 and 9 ranges and kept the sample relatively low in the mix. I have still not made a decision as to whether I will be keeping the sample, imitating it, or just rewriting the musical content.

The drums are pretty much panned how I want them. I have slightly offset the hihats, the ride, and the secondary hihats and kept the 3 kicks all central. This has given some width to the drums and kept the individual elements in sensible pan positions. This is completely dry with no dynamic or effect processing whatsoever.

The mix is starting to take shape now. With all the levels set and the pans slightly altered, I am in a position to now take the mix to the next stage.

Bear in mind I have not applied any effects or dynamics, and have kept all the pans close to centre. The reason I have not made any glaringly huge changes to levels and pans is because I know that when it comes to using dynamics, in particular, I will have gain boosts and gain drops to consider. So, by keeping the levels well below the headroom's ceiling, I can accommo-

Tip

Nothing sounds worse than a badly panned mix.

Sound file

Nelson level and pan mix edited.

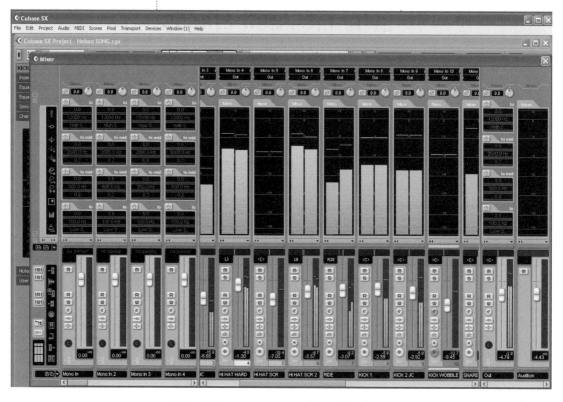

Figure 9.2

date any dramatic changes without blowing my eardrums, speakers and credibility.

I have used the same thinking for the pan settings. Once I start to apply effects, I know that my pan spots will have to be altered. So, by keeping my pans conservative, I am allowing for any sweeping changes that might take place. We will have lots of time later to play around with EQ, compression etc, so keep it simple.

Save the level and pan mix as a file in your sequencer.

Performing the level and pan mix is a really good way to adjust your thinking to the mix process, in stages and in sequence. If you jump straight in and just try to work on a track/channel at a time, then you will get nowhere fast.

This type of process is a great way to attune your ears to the sounds that go into forming the mix. It is also a good way to get your brain to work in a structured order, with emphasis on layout, naming, and grouping.

Always think about what you are doing when it comes to setting levels and pans. Be aware of the frequencies being used and what spaces they occupy.

Now let us start using dynamics and effects.

Tip

As always, keep it clean, keep it simple.

Tip

A good practice is to have your software sequencer set to auto save every few minutes.

Mixing with dynamics and effects

We are now going to be working off the settings in Figure 10.1. As you can see from the peak lines above the metering, I have left ample headroom in the event that the dynamics and effects I use might boost the signals. I always, as you know by now, work from a structured and logical order.

I do not believe in using different compressors on every channel. Prior to the virtual world of mixing, we used to use only a couple of hardware compressors and a mixer, so why start using a multitude of compressors on every channel? Generally, I use one compressor for the drums and one compressor for the overall mix, and only if I need to do so.

In a mix of this nature, where the drums are integral to the genre, I might use two compressors for the drums and one for the singing if the vocal recording is all over the place with peaks and lows and has no sensible dynamic movement.

For effects, I will use the 'old' method of assigning an effect, like reverb, to an auxiliary send and return and working off the aux send on each channel. This

Figure 10.1

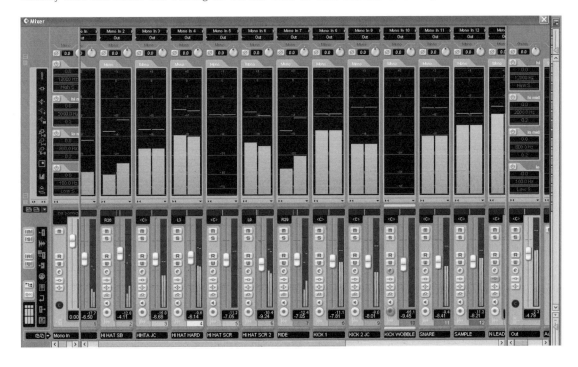

method is excellent for applying the same reverb and its characteristics to any number of channels. There are two reasons why this is a great way to work.

1 Different reverbs have different tonal characteristics (colour). By using the same reverb on the channels, you stick to the same type of tonal colour and the channels all sound uniform.
2 Most reverb plug-ins, particularly SIR reverbs, are CPU hungry. The more plug-ins you have selected and in use, the more you hog the CPU.

Of course, you might want to use certain types of reverbs on certain sounds, and for that you might feel a dedicated reverb plug-in is needed for those particular sounds, say: a gated reverb on a snare. For this you will need more than one instance of a reverb plug-in.

Use your plug-ins sensibly and if you must use a shed load of plug-ins, then make sure you use the 'freeze' function within your sequencer (if you have one). Freeze converts the channels with the active plug-ins into audio tracks and helps to free up resources and plug-ins.

But before we jump into the compressor/reverb pool, let us first use EQ. EQ (equalization) is a great tool for separating and emphasizing frequencies. For the mix I am conducting in this book, I will be using EQ for separating and beefing up the drum sounds, and for adding harmonies to the vocals.

EQ

I love using EQ, simply because it is such a versatile function, and my favourite tool from the dynamics arsenal. Compression is also a major weapon, but I always like to shape the sound with EQ and then bring it to life with compression.

There are debates, on both sides of the fence, as to whether you EQ before compression or after. Both are perfectly acceptable, but you must have a pre conceived idea in your head as to what you want the sound to sound like before you decide which comes first. Take a look at Figure 10.2. The wavy line is the compression curve. The vertical bar lines represent the EQ bands and the height denotes the amplitude or gain applied to those bands (frequencies).

Figure 10.2
Compression curve and EQ bands.

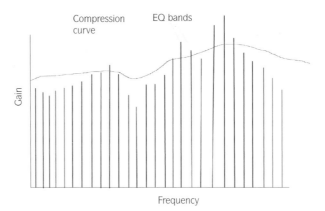

As you can see, the compression curve is smoother and more narrow banded. Using this particular setup, EQ before compression, I can smooth out any major peaks and boost any dips, so as to bring the two together. This method is great for getting the compressed signal to sound how you want it to sound. However, if you can use a compressor and attain the sound you want, then you can apply EQ afterwards to further shape the sound.

If you cannot attain the sound you want with the compressor then use EQ before the compressor to get the final compressed signal to sound how you want it. This can, of course, mean that you are boosting frequencies with the EQ and then cutting those same frequencies with the compressor.

This argument will go on for ages. Personally, I care only about one thing; does it work? At the end of the day, all these tools are exactly that, tools. You use them how you see fit. Music technology has many get-out clauses. You can break many rules and then write a book about it, and then the film and DVD will follow, and before you know it, you are going out with Angelina Jolie.

For this mix, I am going to EQ the drums first. That will then set the tone for the whole mix. Normally, I always start with the vocals. This way, I shape the mix around the vocal content. But in this instance, the vocals are a combination of sung hooks and spit (rap). Because of the genre dictated here, I need to make sure the drums move along nicely with the vocals and bass line.

As I do not have a bass line yet, only a sample with the bass line incorporated in it, I need to consider what will drive this mix. I could use the sample with the inherent bass line, but I not only do not like the sample itself but there are other sounds within the sample that would suffer greatly if I were to EQ, say, the low frequencies.

This type of problem arises almost all the time when samples are used. You have a number of ways of resolving the problem.

- You can imitate the sample by playing the parts within it.
- You can layer the sample with other sounds to mask the frequencies you are going to process.
- You can try to EQ or filter the frequencies that you want to use, or discard, from the sample.
- You can try your best to process the sample as it is.

If you are under contract to perform a mix and not a remix, then you are obligated to use the material exactly as it is provided.

If, on the other hand, you are presented with a contract to mix and produce the content with emphasis on your own input, then there is area for moving away from content you see to be unfit or not 'right' for the mix in question.

Tip

As always let your ears decide.

Using EQ at the mix stage

As we discussed in the previous chapter, I am going to EQ the drums first. This will set the drive of the mix in motion. The genre has dictated that I follow this process first, as opposed to using EQ for the vocals. As the genre is Hip Hop, the drums are crucial to the 'feel' of the mix.

So, let us begin. I always start with the lowest frequencies and work up from there. I have three kicks to EQ in this mix. I also need to consider any other drum sounds that fall in the same frequency range as the kicks. Normally, the bass sound would also be soloed with the kick sound so that the EQ process does not end up creating frequency clashes.

Figure 11.1 shows how I have soloed the three kicks together. Remember when I said to group the necessary instrument sounds together? Well, here is a perfect example as to why grouping relevant and complementary sounds together and next to each other is so important. It makes for easy navigation and editing.

I am now going to select a certain EQ module and also decide on how I want it to appear. Some people like dials, others prefer numerical represen-

Tip

The best way to EQ drums is to solo the drum channels that represent similar frequencies.

Figure 11.1
Three kicks soloed together.

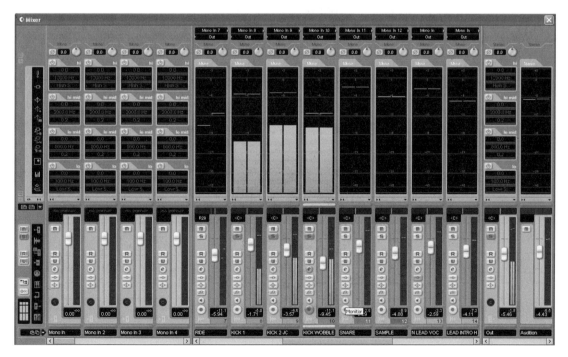

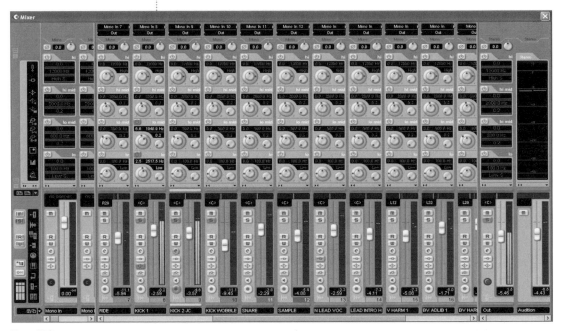

Figure 11.2
EQ applied to the first kick drum.

tation etc. I like dials….pah! There, dials everywhere! I am joyous.

Kicks

Figure 11.2 shows that I have applied some EQ to the first kick drum sound, predominantly in the low to lo-mid frequency ranges. Now, this might be hard for you to digest, as figures are being used, so I will use the audio channel editor (Figure 11.3) to show you how these parameters look in graphical form.

Figure 11.3
Audio edit window.

Sometimes, the graphical display can give you a lot more information that a numerical display, as you can see the shape of the EQ curve on the sound being processed.

Figure 11.3 shows the audio edit window that I have opened. I have placed the graphical representation of the EQ settings I have applied next to the same dial settings in the mixer window. The graph clearly shows where I have applied boosts. Figure 11.4 is a magnification of the EQ section in the audio editor.

Figure 11.4
A magnification of the EQ section in the audio editor.

The figures at the bottom of the graph represent frequencies and the horizontal figures on the vertical axis represent the dB boost (gain). The 1 and 2 represent the EQ modules I have selected from the mixer window, starting from Low (1) to High (4).

The curve that I have created shows that there is a boost at 282 Hz of around 5 dB (low shelving filter) and this is maintained till the next boost stage at 1940.9 Hz with a Q factor of .2 and a boost of 6 dB.

Q, in this instance, denotes a range from Low Shelving Filter when set to minimum at the Low modules, and Low Pass Filter when set to maximum when using the High module. Of course, there are varying stages of this at each module.

Figure 11.5 shows that I have applied an EQ boost around 2069 Hz at 0.2 Q for the second kick. This has afforded me a nice variation on the two kicks, the first one being a deeper and harder kick and the second one being a looser and distorted type of kick.

So far, I have kept the EQ curves quite simple and boosted well above the very low end frequency range of 80 Hz plus. I have also used the EQ lightly because I know that I will be using compression later and this will further define the frequencies.

There is another reason why I have kept the kick EQs around the 1-2 kHz mark. This is to do with separation. EQ is a great tool for separation, and you can clearly define the edges of a sound and boost or cut from the body.

Figure 11.5
EQ boost applied at 0.2 Q.

In this instance, I have chosen to define the edges and low-mid frequencies more than boosting the bodies of the kicks. If I chose to boost the low frequencies then I would have had conflicts between the two main kicks. At 200 or so Hz, I am applying a small boost but not pushing the energy frequencies. This allows me the room to play around with these settings later, when the mix starts to really take shape.

Snare

The snare is next, and Figure 11.6 shows small boosts around the 800 Hz – 2 kHz (both at 0.2 Q) range. The snare sound was quite nice to start with and all it needed was a nicely peaked EQ curve at the usual snare attack/body frequency range. I have left the high end alone and not concentrated too much on the lower end. I have tried to accentuate the snare's attack and part way into the body, to give it that dirty snap whilst maintaining its attack.

Unless it's called for, I generally try to accentuate and define the existing sounds. Only in extreme situations will I substitute a different sound for an existing one.

Remember that the song has already been written and those particular sounds have been chosen. Only if you are producing the mix and have a say over what needs inputting/changing etc, will you be able to change things around. You need to keep within the boundaries set up between you, as the person entrusted with the mix, and the paying customer, who has entrusted you to mix as professionally as possible. Your job is to fulfill all the criteria we have been discussing until now. If the client has given you a snare you don't like, it is not up to you to ditch it and use one that you do like. If you are a producer and given this latitude, then by all means do as you feel is required.

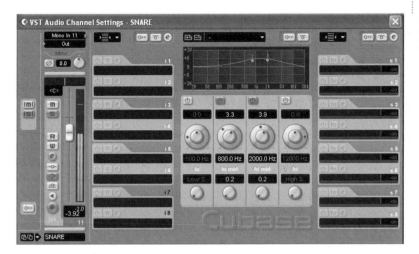

Figure 11.6
Small boosts applied around the
800 Hz – 2 kHz range.

In this instance, you can suggest to the client that a different snare be used. Note the word 'suggest'. Being a paid entity entails diplomacy, not just technical skills and knowledge. Brush up on those skills as much as the music technology ones if you want to make a living in this industry.

> **Tip**
>
> Being a paid entity entails diplomacy, not just technical skills and knowledge.

Working with percussion

When working with percussion, use a sensible sequence of processes. If you have effects or oddball percussive sounds being used in a mix, treat them last in the percussive food chain. Get the damn beat kicking and right, then worry about kick drops or reverse scratches.

Ride

Right, let us go back to the mix. We are now left with the percussive sounds minus the kicks and snare. I think ride and hihats should come next. Because I know that the ride has more in terms of frequency content than the hihats, I have chosen to EQ this next.

When working on the metallic percussive sounds, always work low frequencies upwards, much as we have done with the kicks etc. Applying EQ to dominant sounds like these will have a major impact on the more frequency diminutive sounds like the hihats. We know that a ride will always be longer and fuller than a hihat, that's a given. So, let's work on the 'frequency fillers' first and then make our way to the thinner and more diminutive sounds.

With a mix of this nature, the ride plays a dominant role in the drive of the beat. Do not ignore that. Use the solo function and solo the ride with the snare and make sure they are not clashing in the frequency domain.

If the ride is particularly full, then solo it with the kick as well as the snare and edit it to provide a good frequency spread amongst these particular sounds.

I love rides, but hate badly sampled ones. Often the life is lacking from them and the tails always end abruptly because the person sampling them has not considered the merits of long sustains, or has simply compromised on file size, or is just bad at what he/she does.

I also find that too many rides used in music nowadays sound very artificial. Either they have not been recorded well, with consideration to space,

> **Tip**
>
> The more frequencies covered by a sound, the more you have to be aware of its place in the stereo field.

ambience or the acoustical tonal qualities of a ride, or they have been pro-grammed to death thus squeezing the life out them through too many dynamic processes. Sounds like rides need to be respected and brought into play in a mix for the sake of realism and frequency spread.

The ride that I am confronted with is not too bad but lacks real body and sounds a little too metallic. I will be concentrating on the lo-mid to hi-mid fre-quency range for the EQ application. I am not too bothered with its attack as there are other percussive components in the beat that will enhance it nice-ly by layering themselves onto the attack.

The decay is adequate and does not need to be too long as the BPM of the mix is a good enough BPM that decays do not sound cut-off. Had this been a slower tempo and more jazz orientated, then the tail would have had to be extended. However, it's not in the 'short' domain and is workable. It is the body I am hoping to define and accentuate. This is why I have chosen those particular frequency ranges to work with.

If you listen carefully to the two audio files listed left, you will hear the dif-ferences in the tonal qualities. They are very subtle, but are enough to add body to the ride. Sometimes, it's these small changes that make the differ-ence between a good sound and a bad sound.

Sound files

Ride no EQ
EQ Ride

Figure 11.7
Audio channel settings for the ride.

Hihats

Next up, we have the standard hihats, dirty hihats and small open hihat to consider. I will treat all the six hihats together and then solo all of them, along with the ride, and listen to them collectively. I am not going to go into indi-vidual EQ settings for each but will include the image for all of them in the mixer window, so you can view the settings for yourself.

Setting EQ curves for hihats is very dependent on the way the whole drum beat sits and what focus the writer or producer takes for the overall feel of the beat.

- Some producers like to have the hihats in your face and up front.
- Some like them sizzling and panned all over the place.
- Others like them hard and behind the snare etc.

There are so many variations that you can use. The main goal should be to make the hihats sound as natural as possible and to use them to enhance the body of the overall beat.

The only instances when I really concentrate on hihats as dominant sounds is when they are used sparsely, and in particular Hip Hop mixes where the hihat presence is essential and quite often as forward as the snare. In this instance, the hihats are there to form the body of the beat, more as fillers than anything else. They give the beat bounce, and a little variation that keeps the listener interested.

As you can see (Figure 11.8), the only hihat sound not affected by EQ is the hihat scratch. All the others have boosts and cuts. The aim is to find a rounded and full frequency spread across all the individual hihats so that, together, they form a unified feel.

Sound files

Hihats no EQ
EQ hihats

Figure 11.8

If you listen to the hihats together you will notice subtle changes and no dramatic processing has taken place. You will also notice that I have accentuated one of the hihats that sits on the same beat as the snare. I have done this to add some snap to the attack of the snare sound when played together.

Sound files

Ride and hihats together

Vocals

Now we come to the vocals. The vocals are the most complicated of sounds to EQ as they cover such a vast frequency spectrum, and each voice is unique in tonal characteristics, and delivery (how a singer sings) also needs to be taken into consideration when processing.

The procedure is a little more complicated in application. You need to concentrate on getting the lead vocal absolutely right, because, if the lead vocal

Tip

The vocals are the most complicated of sounds to EQ as they cover such a vast frequency spectrum, and each voice is unique in tonal characteristics and delivery (how a singer sings) also needs to be taken into consideration when processing.

doesn't sound right, then all the other vocals will also sound wrong as they will be processed relative to how the lead vocal sounds.

Most producers have more problems in this department than any other. The most common being: how to express the delivery of the vocals and how to fit them in the frequency spectrum without encountering clashes or masking.

The vocals I have here are a combination of the 'spit' (rap), the backing vocals, harmonies and intros and outros. The problem I am faced with is that the recording of the vocals was not very good and there are some quite distinct level changes across each channel, so I will either need to automate the gains or run a compressor across the channels that have the level problems.

The other problem I am faced with is that each track has been recorded with a combination of different vocal lines, meaning that not only is there the spit on a track but also harmonies. This has happened because the person performing the spit and some of the harmonies has decided (or the engineer has) to record right through the whole song and add bits in on the same track as the song is progressing. This is poor recording technique.

A good engineer would make sure that the spit is on one track, separate from the harmonies and backing vocals. You must always keep these elements separate on different tracks.

If there are adlibs, then have one track dedicated to them. If there are backing vocals, then keep those on a different track, unless there are more than one backing vocals, then you must use more tracks. I could go on, but I believe you get the picture.

It is better to have more tracks of vocal recordings than to try to put them on a couple of tracks. This makes mixing a nightmare. I have come across engineers that will record separate drum parts across multiple channels but devote two channels for all the vocals.

It makes perfect sense to separate the styles and techniques on separate channels. I might need to use a certain reverb on the backing vocals but not on the lead. If both vocals have been recorded on the same track, then I have a problem. Of course, I can edit each track and assign separate tracks to each part within that track, but had the recording been done sensibly then this would not be necessary.

I could also choose to automate the effects and gains, but this would require considerably more time and effort than necessary had the vocals been recorded sensibly.

As we discussed earlier, your job is to mix already recorded material, but if the material is so badly recorded, then that leaves you having to correct errors and restore quality. That makes the project far more time consuming and inevitably more costly. I often reject mixes because of poor recordings and multiple error files.

Back to the mix. As with the drums, solo the vocals and listen to them. The audio example shows: the corrective noise removal we performed earlier, the levels between all the different vocal parts and light gain settings for all the parts.

The vocal section sounds well balanced with the lead spit standing dominant and the harmonies not dwarfing the spit. The backing vocals are also set to add just the right gain to the rest of the vocals without washing them over.

Sound files

Vocals panned and levels

Figure 11.9
Vocals panned and levels.

The pan settings have helped to provide just enough width and have helped in positioning the vocals in their correct places in the stereo field. These are:

- Lead vocals – central.
- Backing vocals – behind and to the sides.
- Harmonies – used in layering the lead, and also placed to the sides when layering the backing vocals.

Now let us use EQ to further define the vocals. There are two areas of process here:

- The first entails using EQ to thicken and layer harmonies and backing vocals
- The second entails separating vocals and using extreme EQ to create harmonies of an existing vocal part.

In this instance, I am not going to use EQ to create harmonies as I already have the recorded harmonies. But if you had very little in the way of vocal harmonies, then you could, for example, create two copies of the lead vocal and apply low end EQ to one layer and high end EQ to the other and add all three together.

You could even offset (delay) the two copies ever so slightly to give a slight phase effect. This will give the perception of thickness and more naturally sung vocals than a dead-on accurate layer.

For this mix, I have enough vocal parts to play with. However, I will use EQ to add a bit of definition to the parts. Let's start with the lead vocal.

Figure 11.10

Lead vocals and drums soloed.

Figure 11.10 shows that I have soloed the lead vocal along with all the drum parts. I have done this because I am working off a beat driven genre (Hip Hop) with the spit being integral to the mix. So, with this thinking, I have made sure to work out all the frequency spreads between these two crucial elements.

Figure 11.11 shows the EQ curve I have set. It is a gentle curve that does not boost or cut any specific frequency range. The vocal file provided had adequate frequency spread and did not need too much treatment. However, it does need a little definition, and this is due to the drum beat's frequency spread. The boosts have been centered on the low-mid to high frequency ranges, and have been limited to no more than 5 dB.

Figure 11.11

Boosts have been centered on the low-mid to high frequency ranges.

Figures 11.12 to 11.14 show the EQ curves I have set for the processed vocals.

Figure 11.12
Outro Vocals

Figure 11.13
BV Harmony 1

Figure 11.14
BV Adlib 1

The EQ curves for the vocals have all been set to complement the lead vocal line. I have taken the drums as my reference point for the vocal EQ curves and I have a relatively full and well spread frequency spectrum. Have a listen to the sound file for the vocals and drums together.

And finally, we are left with the sample. This particular sample is troublesome, as mentioned earlier, and there is a vocal line within the main sample that needs to be heard in the mix, and the main sample has a string hook that covers the frequency of the vocal line, so if I try to EQ the string, I end up processing the vocal line as well. The main sample is also low frequency heavy so any adjustments at this frequency range also affect the vocal and string frequencies.

I am going to try to use a few EQ modules to accent the vocal line and abate the rest (Figure 11.15).

Figure 11.15
EQing the sample.

As you can hear from the sound file, I have tried to keep the vocal line as prominent as possible in the main sample. The strings have been strongly peaked (over 20 dB) at around 1 kHz but with a strong drop down to nearer the 10 kHz range. The image shows a 17 dB drop from 1 kHz down to 10 kHz. I have done this to take the edge off the higher frequencies in relation to the mid and lower frequencies. The EQ curve clearly shows this.

By processing the main sample this way, I have allowed the lower frequencies to be taken up by the vocals and the drums. This sounds cleaner than the deep and muddy bass sound that exists in the main sample.

Of course, when it comes to completing the mix, I am sure that certain frequencies will get boosted again, predominantly after I use compression. I have allowed for this with the way I have sculpted the EQ curve across the main sample.

Now, let us move onto compression.

Compression in the mix

We have looked in detail at what a compressor is used for and how to use it. We now need to consider its place in this particular mix.

I like to use compressors for further defining a sound in a mix. A compressor can bring a sound out nicely in a mix and is often used for this purpose. I do not like to use compression as a means to gain as much loudness as possible. I prefer to use a compressor to define a sound and to use it on the master stereo mix to have control over the dynamics.

What I hate, and advise everyone to stop doing, is when a compressor is used to try to make a mix as loud as possible. This process often ends up squashing the life out of the mix leaving no discernable dynamic peaks and troughs.

A badly compressed file of this nature always exhibits square shaped envelopes instead of smooth peaks, a tell tale sign of an over compressed file.

The way I use compressors in a virtual mixer is by assigning the relevant channels to a group that I have created as a channel to house the compressor. This saves space and does not tax the CPU. If you had to use the same compressor on each channel that you wanted to compress, it would then hog your CPU.

In Cubase I have created a group channel and called it 'D Comp' (Drum Compressor). I can then select which channels I want assigned to the group channel.

In the case of the drums, I will be assigning all the drum channels I want to compress to the D Comp group channel and that way I only need to use one instance of the compressor vst, and thus freeing the computer of valuable processing power etc.

Figure 12.1 shows that I have selected the snare channel and am about to set its output to the group channel that I have named 'D Comp'. This group channel can clearly be seen at the end of the mixer channels. You can create more group channels if you need to.

For this particular project, I am assigning the chosen drum channels to the D Comp channel. This way, I can compress any/all the drum sounds as a whole. But certain drum sounds need to be compressed with specific settings to make the overall beat sound as you want it to. In this case, it would pay to use separate compressors on separate channels.

However, you need to be aware that the more plug-ins you use, the more taxing it will be for your computer.

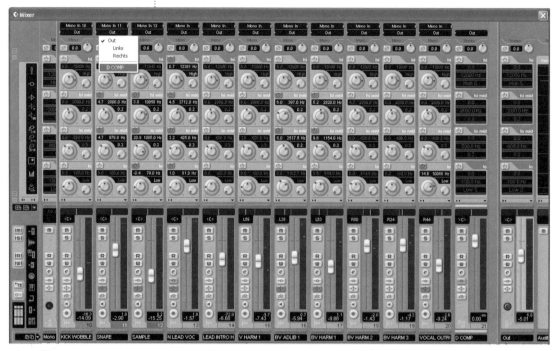

Figure 12.1
I have selected the snare channel and am about to set its output to the group channel that I have named 'D Comp'

Figure 12.2
Load a multiband compressor.

Now, let us load a compressor into the group channel. I have chosen a multiband compressor as the drum compressor for the selected group channel. I find that a multiband compressor is a very good compressor to use as I can compress different frequency bands, separate from each other. In other words, I can compress the different drum sounds together without worrying

about shared frequencies being compressed, as I can define which frequencies need compressing and by what parameters.

As the drum beat is already pretty much how I want it to sound, I have decided that the areas that would probably benefit the most from compression is the main kick drum, secondary kick and the snare.

I want to leave the hihats and ride as they are as the EQ curves I created and used already defined the percussive elements to pretty much near to what I want them to sound like. They are also not too variable on gain, so I don't really need to apply compression for gain control. I also do not want to have to boost them in any way whatsoever, as they are already sitting pretty in the mix.

The kicks and snare need a little 'oomph', so let's get to work. Figure 12.3 shows the type of settings I have used for the drum compression.

Figure 12.3
Settings used for drum compression.

Normally, I would use the Waves C1 compressor in Cubase, but I have chosen the multiband as it has more parameters that can be used and it is these parameters that I want you to think about.

The low, mid and high bands are defined by the frequency crossover bands f1, f2, f3 and f4. These can be set to define each frequency's start and end points and the crossover points. These bands make up the low, mid and high bands. The rest of the parameters should be obvious to you by now as we have covered these in an earlier chapter.

Using the above, you can see how I have set the frequency band parameters. This helps me to define the low, mid and high frequencies. I have been specific in choosing the ranges that I need for the kicks and the snare.

The figures above are only guides as each sound has its own characteristics, so using them for your kicks and snares probably won't be of great help.

However, by understanding what I am doing and the ballpark figures I am using, you will form a better understanding of how compression should be used. Subtly!

There are many types of compressors available nowadays as plug-ins for your sequencer. Figure 12.4 shows another multiband compressor that depicts these parameters in both blocks and graphical formats.

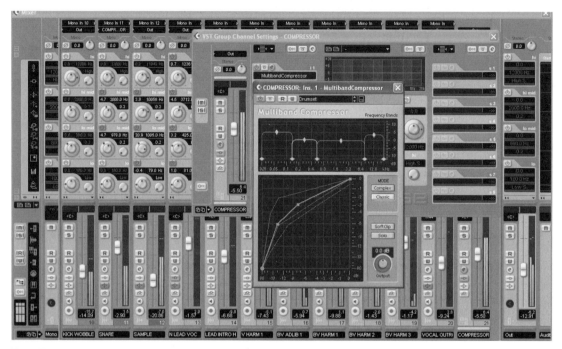

Figure 12.4
A multiband compresspr that uses both blocks and graphical formats

This particular compressor's GUI and interface makes for easy editing. Not only can you see the frequency band areas, but you can resize them (height and width) to suit your needs. Height depicts amplitude and the width is the frequency range. Of course, as simple as it looks, it does present some detailed editing tools.

In the virtual world, the processor's performance is based on how well it is coded and how detailed and good the algorithms are. I tend to find that software based compressors do not really exhibit any tonal colour or imprint their own characteristics onto a signal. This can be a good thing as transparency is what we are generally after with master mix compression.

Hardware compressors can be coloured and this is why certain hardware compressors cost a fortune as they impart their own characteristics onto a signal. Others are transparent but perform the processing extremely well, and that accounts for the pricing as much as the cost of hardware and build etc. I find a combination of the two works wonders.

Now I will create another group channel for the vocals, and this time I will run all the vocals through this channel, so that I can have control over some of the jumps and drops in the gains.

Take a look at Figure 12.5, it is a snapshot of the Waves C1 compressor. It is displaying the vocals that I have grouped together to one compressor.

Tip

Although all of these software based compressors offer tons of variety in terms of interfaces and tools, you only need to consider how well they do the job.

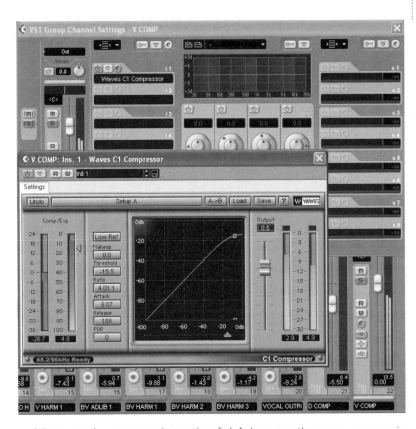

Figure 12.5
Settings used for drum compression.

I have used a compression ratio of 4.1 because there are some gain boosts that need to be tamed, but all else has been kept quite soft as I do not want to have too much influence over the vocal's dynamics. I do not want to change the tonal colour of the vocals or to 'pump' them as I would with a heavy drum beat. The process I am applying is more 'corrective processing', to bring in line the peaks and dips and to keep them in a dynamic band.

Generally, I start off by observing how high the peaks of the vocals hit in bypass mode. I then choose a 'general' ratio setting of 2.1. With vocals, I tend to start off with the attack at about 5 milliseconds (ms) and the release at about 150 milliseconds (ms). I then set the threshold so that the compressor shows a gain reduction at between 4-10 dB. I then adjust the output until the compressed signal's peaks match the bypassed signal's peaks. Even though they share the same peak values, the compressed sound will sound a little livelier.

Of course, all of the above is down to experimentation and, as always, let the ears decide what's good and what isn't.

With regards to the mix we are conducting here, I have found that the spit and one of the backing vocals carry most of the jumps and dips in the gains, so I have used these extremes as the boundaries for the compressor to compress and boost.

This has happened because of poor miking technique. The singer is not compensating for the gain variances by moving away from the mic, or getting closer to it, so we use a compressor to bring in line the extremities of

Tip

Sometimes, I will even mix in the dry unprocessed signal in with the compressed signal (parallel compression). This can give some good results.

the gains and dips. Everything else in between these extremities stays unaffected. This will keep all the vocals in line and bring the peaks and dips closer together to allow for a more natural miking technique.

Only in cases where there is a big difference in gains or the vocals are sung by different people, will I resort to compression on individual channels. For our mix here, the vocals are all sung by the same person, so the characteristics and delivery are the same for all the vocal files.

Always consider the tonal quality of what you are compressing so as to determine the best approach in dynamic management. You need to apply this same analogy to all processes in the technical world of audio processing.

At every point of the mix process, try to use the bypass buttons, for both EQ and compression, to check how the mix sounds processed and unprocessed. I tend to use very little, if any, compression on the master stereo mix. I find that if I have been sensible and accurate in my compressing stages, then I will not need to compress the final mix. I cannot tell you how fed up I get looking at overly compressed mixes and seeing the life squeezed out of the waveform. It's equally bad to listen to.

If sensible and light compression has been used on individual tracks, then running a master compressor on the main mix is not that bad, but advised against.

The processes that I have gone through with you have been of small changes, and in stages, and the results have so far been good.

Compression for master stereo mix

As I explained earlier, it is better to use the compressor in sensible and subtle amounts, and this is most important when using compression to compress the final stereo mix.

A stereo mix will have already been mixed with dynamic movement in mind and if you were to compress heavily, then you would undo all the good work you have done in creating the dynamic peaks and dips. You would, in effect, destroy the peaks and dips and basically squash the life out of the mix.

What most people do not seem to understand is that a mix that is overly compressed is tiring to the ears. Because the energy of the song is narrow banded, the ears become tired with the monotony of this band.

The ears and brain need variety and movement in sound to keep interested. Anything that is narrow banded will have the opposite effect and be sterile in animation.

Use the compressor sensibly and the song will sound louder and more flowing than if you were to compress it to death.

Tip

Compressing a compressed signal makes for poor technical skills.

Tip

Running multiple instances of heavy compression on individual channels and then heavy compression on the final master mix degrades the audio signal and serves no useful purpose at all.

Effects in the mix

Using effects is as important as any other process when it comes to mixing. Effects can add certain qualities to a mix that dynamics cannot. As far as we are concerned regarding this particular mix, reverb is what I want to explore with you. There are two types of effects that reverbs are used for:

- Colour
- Space

Colour
This means that the reverb is being used to add an effect to the sound. An example of this would be to add reverb to a guitar sound to make it sound more rich, wet and washy.

Space
This means that the reverb is being used to give the perception of space. An example of this would be to add reverb to a guitar sound to make it sound as if it is being played in a specific room, like a concert hall. Whether you are using reverb for colour or space, the functionality is the same.

I tend to use certain reverbs because of the tonal qualities they impart onto the signal being treated, and because of this, certain makes and models have become synonymous with the 'colour' or 'transparency' they provide.

Reverbs are the most used and possibly the most potent of all effects. Their parameters are easy to use but it is amazing how many people misuse these parameters. Most people will use the presets on a reverb plug-in and then use the decay and mix parameters to get the effect they want. What they do not realize is that pre-delay and diffusion are two of the most potent parameters available on a reverb unit. By using these two parameters sensibly, you can determine the size of space and how the reflections behave in that given space.

We have discussed what these do already, so I expect you to have an idea as to what I am talking about. Today, we have all manner of reverb plug-ins, and they have all taken the concept of these parameters to another level. We now have 3-D, graphically edited, 'node moving in a box' type of reverb plug-ins etc. But most interesting of all, and the ones that I use nowadays, are Impulse Responses (IR). These are called convolution reverbs, otherwise known as 'sampling' reverbs.

These IRs do not have to be limited to reverbs. They can be IRs from compressors, preamps etc, and just about any effect.

The reverb IRs provide the sounds of real acoustic spaces that are far more realistic than most reverb effects. Each of these spaces or devices is encapsulated into what is called an 'impulse response' file that can be loaded into a compatible convolution playback device. Such devices range from freeware PC and Mac plug-ins to dedicated hardware reverb processors.

Because of the nature of having to record these IRs, most people will be more than happy to simply stick to IRs provided with the playback device, or purchased separately as IRs. In fact, there are literally hundreds of free IRs floating around on the internet, and so long as you have a playback device that can load and play back the IRs, you have unlimited variety to keep you busy.

I do not want to go into how you record IRs as there are countless articles freely available on this very subject.

What I do want to point out is that IRs eat up CPU power as they are often quite long files and processing them can really eat into your CPU power. The shorter files tend to suffer from cut off tails, if recorded poorly.

Another problem encountered with some playback devices is that they can only play back the IRs and not offer any real editing potential. So, it helps to get good quality IRs, that are recorded well and not truncated with short tails, and a decent playback device that has editing potential.

I have also found that many people will use multiple instances of IRs in a mix, by using the playback device loaded with a different IR on each channel. This will drag your computer down to a slow death. I think that in many cases, people actually do not understand how to use a reverb effect plug-in, and end up using it as an insert on a channel. If you are using the same reverb effect, then it makes sense to use it as an auxiliary effect much as we do when using hardware analogue mixers. This allows us to use one master effect and to tap into it using each channel's aux sends. However, you need to check with your sequencer's manual on how to set up a reverb effect as an aux send/return.

For those that have Cubase, here is the process: Right-click on an existing track/channel in the Inspector, and add an FX Channel Track. When the dialog window appears, make the track stereo, and then choose the reverb plug-in you want.

Once this track is available it will appear at the right hand end of the Cubase mixer. Now, to use this as a send on any number of other tracks, open up the Channel Settings window, click on one of the empty send boxes (the six slots down the right hand side) and select the reverb plug-in option for the bus, click the On button, make sure that reverb plug-in is set to all wet, and you are done. Oh, and by the way, next to that 'On' button is a Pre/Post fader button for the Send, if you need it. You cannot get easier than that!

Figure 13.1 shows how it will look. As you can see, I have chosen Voxengo Pristine Space (VPS) as my reverb module.

I can now tap into this plug-in and use any amount of the reverb I want on any channel. Pah, cool or cool? And just to make things a little sweeter for you, have a look at Figure 13.2. It shows you the main panel for VPS and how to load an IR. I have even loaded an IR so that you can see how it looks. I am not going to get into the functionality of this particular reverb module. I just wanted you to see how one uses IRs in a playback device.

By using a reverb on the master auxiliary, you limit the CPU drain and it

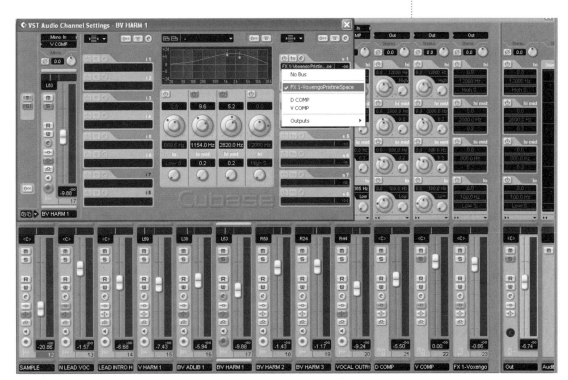

allows you to use the reverb on any number of channels and, as an added bonus, frees up the channel inserts so that you can use any additional effects/dynamics. *But*, it is the CPU that benefits the most from this set up.

Figure 13.1

Figure 13.2

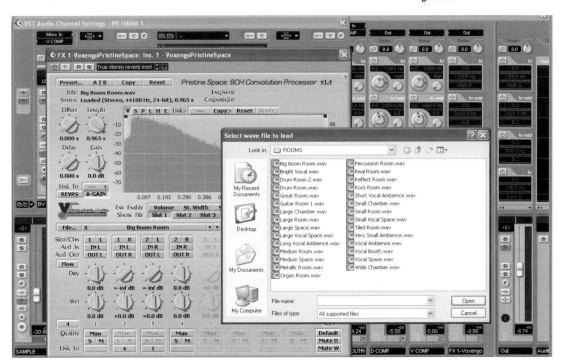

Tip

We have a saying in this industry; 'Less is more'. That saying, although universal, is absolutely accurate when it comes to music.

Back to the mix

I find that using small amounts of reverb on vocals makes for some great ambience. It opens up the different vocal lines and affords them space and the perception is that each vocal is separate from each other but unified as they share the same space.

Less is more

A bad mistake is to use different reverb modules on different vocal channels within the same mix, as each reverb module will have its own tonal characteristic so will colour the sound it is applied to. We have a saying in this industry; 'Less is more'. That saying, although universal, is absolutely accurate when it comes to music.

Most beginners make the mistake of assuming the more of an effect or dynamic that you use, the better the resultant sound will sound. This is wrong, plain and simple.

The brain is amazing, it can sense minute changes in visual and audio. It also has the gift of being able to glean a result from very little information. Using small amounts of reverb will not go amiss. The brain will know what is happening and accommodate it. Speakers/monitors, however, are not so forgiving. Make a mistake and the monitoring system will not only pick up on it, but will amplify it and expose the mistake.

You have seen how I work. I use small amounts when editing and work in sequence. The small amounts, once added, will form a far better and sincere result than slapping on masses of an effect and then trying to carve away at it when it comes to auditioning the final mix.

This particular mix was recorded with room ambience. This has made my job a little harder. Normally, I receive the vocals dry. That allows me to treat them with a reverb of my choosing. If the vocals have been recorded with the natural ambience of a room, then I have to find a reverb that matches the room characteristics or I need to remove the ambience from the vocals.

Tip

Some people record in their bathrooms at home because they like the reflective sound generated by the tiles. I always advise that vocals be recorded as dry as possible. This makes it easier to treat them.

These particular vocals have been recorded in a room that is not too reflective. Some people record in their bathrooms at home because they like the reflective sound generated by the tiles. I always advise that vocals be recorded as dry as possible. This makes it easier to treat them.

Once you have the vocals ready for processing, it is always a good idea to work from the lead vocals onwards, as we have discussed earlier. I like to work on the lead vocal and the secondary vocal that might accompany the lead vocal, as it does in this mix. There is the spit and the accompanying interchange with the secondary vocal. By soloing these two together you have a better idea of placement and how much reverb to apply. Always bear in mind that the lead vocal is king, and that everything else should work to accentuate it.

Creating the sense of space with reverb is an old and tried method, and works extremely well, but it does require that you understand how reverb works and how to use its functions.

By using patterns of closely spaced reverb delays in the left and right channels, you can approximate the way sound bounces around in a real space, and thereby create a sense of width and depth. However, it has to be carefully used, because increasing the overall sense of width and depth in this way can make it increasingly hard to localise the actual sounds themselves.

One way of reducing the blurring of the stereo image by reverb is to use a mono reverb for some sounds, as discussed earlier, and then pan the reverb return to the same position. This is exactly the method I am using for this particular mix.

I have included two versions of the same mix, one has sensible amounts of reverb and the other has too much reverb.

As you will hear, the one that has too much reverb has created pan problems and too much muddying of the sounds. The problem with this is that we have now lost definition between the sounds and because the reverb has a lot of shared transients when in use; the sounds have marred EQ curves. This is exactly what we do not want. We have gone to all that trouble to place, define and present the sounds and now we have wrecked it with a simple error like using too much reverb.

I cannot stress how important it is to recognize the failings of these types of practices. Beginners often feel they have to 'wash' the mix with reverb to attain space. This is nonsense. Clever use of reverb assures a spatial mix with natural reflections where needed.

Certain genres will ask for more in the way of effects, and using reverbs and delays is the basis for most Trance based music. That is acceptable, because this genre is defined by the effects it uses.

Always consider the bigger picture and how *all* the sounds sit in a mix. Think about the space all the sounds occupy. If you apply too much reverb on one vocal channel and much less on another, do you think it will then sound natural, as if the vocalists are in the same room?

To conclude, I would like you to listen to the two short concluding audio files. A mix with low reverb and a mix with too much reverb. Which do you prefer?

Conclusion

I hope this book has been of help to you. I am aware that these types of tutorials can serve to better explain the content as they encompass visual and audio examples. As with all of my tutorials, I have tried to keep a detached approach to the content, considering the reader's viewpoint. With this in mind, I have tried to explain the content as I would explain it to a friend in a chat over a few beers. Please try to apply the content to your own situation and follow the advice as it is presented.

Music is about fun, but it is also a highly technical vocation. Treat it exactly as that. Master the technical aspects and enjoy the fun bits, because if you cannot do both then you need another vocation. If you are a hobbyist and have no inclination to join this mad industry, then please try to use the information in this book as it will help you to understand the thinking and procedures behind the content.

But most of all enjoy!

Zukan (Eddie Bazil)

Samplecraze

Tip

One way of reducing the blurring of the stereo image by reverb is to use a mono reverb for some sounds, as discussed earlier, and then pan the reverb return to the same position.

Sound file

Mix with low reverb.
Mix with too much reverb.

Index